EXCEL 2000
Core

Excel and Windows are registered trademarks of Microsoft Corporation. All other trademarks quoted are the property of their respective editors.

All rights reserved. No part of this publication may be reproduced, stored in a retrieval system, or transmitted, in any form, or by any means, electronic, mechanical, photocopying, recording or otherwise, without the prior permission of the publishers.

Copyright - Editions ENI - February 2000
ISBN: 2-7460-0886-6
Original edition: 2-7460-0870-X

Editions ENI

BP 32125
44021 NANTES Cedex 1

Tel. 02.51.80.15.15
Fax 02.51.80.15.16

e-mail: editions@ediENI.com
http://www.editions-eni.com

ENI Publishing LTD

500 Chiswick High Road
London W4 5RG

Tel. 020 8956 2320
Fax 020 8956 2321

e-mail: publishing@ediENI.com
http://www.editions-eni.com

Collection directed by Corinne HERVO

MOUS
Excel 2000 Core

INTRODUCTION 3

EXCEL 2000
1.1 Overview 11

WORKBOOKS AND WORKSHEETS
2.1 Workbooks 21
2.2 Worksheets 39

ROWS, COLUMNS AND CELLS
3.1 Rows/Columns 53
3.2 Cells 65

MANAGING DATA
4.1 Entering data 73
4.2 Modifying data 83
4.3 Copying and moving 93

CALCULATIONS

5.1 Formulas 105
5.2 Functions 115

PRESENTATION OF DATA

6.1 Formatting data 129
6.2 Styles 151

PRINTING

7.1 Printing 157
7.2 Page Setup 169

DRAWING OBJECTS

8.1 Charts 181
8.2 Drawing objects 203

SUMMARY EXERCISES 215

TABLE OF OBJECTIVES 226

INDEX 231

MOUS
Excel 2000 Core

This book is the ideal tool for an effective preparation of the Excel 2000 Core exam. The MOUS logo on the cover guarantees that this edition has been approved by Microsoft®. It contains the theoretical information corresponding to all the topics tested in the exam and you can test your knowledge by working through the practice exercises. If you succeed in completing these exercises without any difficulty, you are ready to take your exam. At the end of the book, you can see a list of the Excel 2000 Core exam objectives, and the number of the lesson and exercise that refer to each of these objectives.

What is the MOUS certification?

The MOUS (Microsoft Office User Specialist) exam gives you the opportunity to obtain a meaningful certification, recognised by Microsoft®, for the Office applications: Word, Excel, Access, PowerPoint, and Outlook. This certification guarantees your level of skill in working with these applications. It can provide a boost to your career ambitions, as it proves that you can use effectively all the features of the Microsoft Office applications and thus offer a high productivity level to your employer. In addition, it is a certain plus when job-seeking: more and more companies require employment candidates to be MOUS certificate holders.

What are the applications concerned?

You can gain MOUS certification in Office 97 applications (Word, Excel, PowerPoint and Access) and in Office 2000 applications (Word, Excel, PowerPoint, Access and Outlook). MOUS exams also exist for Word 7 and Excel 7. Two exam levels are offered for Word 97, Word 2000, Excel 97 and Excel 2000: a Core level (proficiency) and a second Expert level. For PowerPoint 97 and Access 97, only the Expert certification is available. For PowerPoint 2000, Access 2000 and Outlook 2000, only one level of certification is available.

If you obtain the Expert level for Word 97, Excel 97, PowerPoint 97 and Access 97, you are certified as a Master in Office 97. If you obtain the Expert level for Word 2000 and Excel 2000 as well as MOUS certification in PowerPoint 2000, Access 2000 and Outlook 2000, you are certified as a Master in Office 2000.

INTRODUCTION
What is MOUS?

How do you apply to sit the exams?

To enrol for the exams, you should contact one of the Microsoft Authorized Testing Centers (or ATC). A list of these centres is available online at this address: http://www.mous.net. There is also http://www.mous.edexcel.org.uk specifically for the UK. Make sure you know the version of the Office application for which you wish to obtain the certificate (is it the 97 or 2000 version?).

There is an enrolment fee for each exam.

On the day of the exam, you should carry some form of identification and, if you have already sat a MOUS exam, your ID number.

What happens during the MOUS exam?

During the exam, you will have a computer that you must use to perform a certain number of tasks on the software in question. Each action you perform to carry out these tasks will be tested in order to make sure that you have done correctly what was asked of you. There are no multiple-choice questions and the exam is not a simulation; you work directly in the application (Word, Excel…).

You are allowed no notes, books, pencils or calculators during the exam. You can consult the application help, but you should be careful not to exceed the exam's time limit.

Each exam is timed; it lasts in general between 45 minutes and one hour.

How do you pass the exam?

You must carry out a certain percentage of the required tasks correctly, within the allocated time. This percentage varies depending on the exam.

You will be told your result as soon as you have finished your exam. These results are confidential (the data are coded) and are only made known to the candidate and to Microsoft.

What happens then?

You will receive a Microsoft-approved exam certificate, proving that you hold the specified MOUS (Microsoft Office User Specialist) level.

What happens if I fail?

You will be given the list of tasks that were not performed correctly, so you see where you went wrong. You can take the exam as many times as you like, but will have to pay the enrolment fee again each time you apply.

INTRODUCTION
How this book works

How this book works

This book is the ideal companion to an effective preparation of the **MOUS Excel 2000 Core** exam. It is divided into several sections, each containing one or more **chapters**. Each section deals with a specific topic: managing workbooks and worksheets, modifying rows, columns and cells in a worksheet, entering and editing text and values, making various calculations, formatting tables, printing, drawing and working with drawing objects. Each chapter is independent from the others. You can tailor the training to suit you: if you already know how to format data, for example, you can skip this lesson and go straight to the practice exercise for that chapter, then if you feel you need some extra theory, you can look back at the relevant points in the lesson. You can also study the lessons and/or work through the exercises in any order you wish.

At the end of the book, there is an **index** to help you find the explanations for any action, whenever you need them.

From theory...

Each chapter starts with a **lesson** on the theme in question and the lesson is made up of a variable amount of numbered topics. The lesson should supply you with all the theoretical information necessary to acquire that particular skill. Example screens to illustrate the point discussed enhance the lesson and you will also find tips, tricks and remarks to complement the explanations provided.

...To practice

Test your knowledge by working through the **practice exercise** at the end of each chapter: each numbered heading corresponds to an exercise question. A solution to the exercise follows. These exercises are done using the documents on the CD-ROM accompanying the book, that you install on your own computer (to see how, refer to the INSTALLING THE CD-ROM instructions). In addition to the chapter exercises, seven **summary exercises** dealing with each of the section themes are included at the end of the book. The solutions to these exercises appear as documents on the CD-ROM.

All you need to succeed!

When you can complete all the practice exercises without any hesitation or problems, you are ready to sit the MOUS exam. In the table of contents for each chapter, the topics corresponding to a specific exam objective are marked with this symbol: ▦. At the back of the book, you can also see **the official list of the Excel 2000 Core exam objectives** and for each of these objectives the corresponding lesson and exercise number.

INTRODUCTION
How this book works

The layout of this book

This book is laid out in a specific way with special typefaces and symbols so you can find all the information you need quickly and easily:

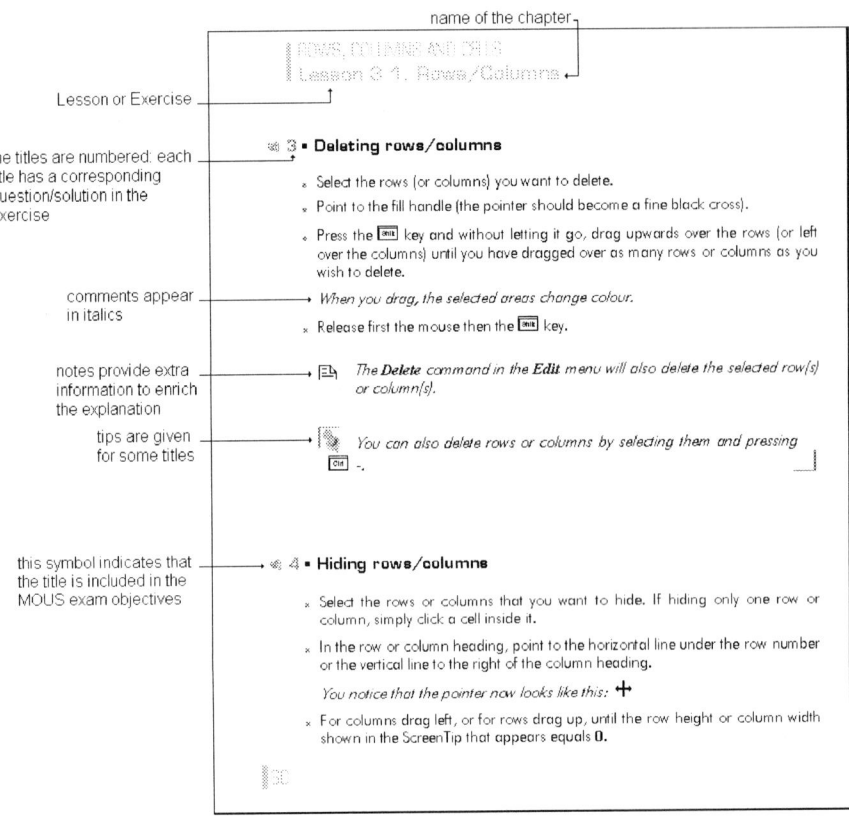

You can tell whether an action should be performed with the mouse, the keyboard or with the menu options by referring to the symbol that introduces each action: 🖱, 🎲 and 📄.

Installing the CD-ROM

The CD-ROM provided contains the documents used to work through the practice exercises and the summary exercise solutions. When you follow the installation procedure set out below, a folder called MOUS Excel 2000 is created on your hard disk and the CD-ROM documents are decompressed and copied into the created folder. The CD-ROM also contains a template which you should copy into the Excel Templates folder.

- Put the CD-ROM into the CD-ROM drive of your computer.
- Start the Windows Explorer: click the **Start** button, point to the **Programs** option then click **Windows Explorer**.
- In the left pane of the Explorer window, scroll through the list until the CD-ROM drive icon appears. Click this icon.

  The contents of the CD-ROM appear in the right pane of the Explorer window.

- Double-click the icon of the **MOUS Excel 2000** folder in the right pane of the Explorer window.

  *The **MOUS Excel 2000** dialog box appears.*

- Click **Next**.

  The installation application offers to create a folder called MOUS Excel 2000.

- Modify the proposed folder name if you wish then click **Next**. If several people are going to be doing the practice exercises on the same computer, you should modify the folder name so each person is working on their own copy of the folder.

INTRODUCTION
Installing the CD-ROM

- Click **Yes** to confirm creating the **MOUS Excel 2000** folder.

    The installation application decompresses the documents then copies them into the created folder.

- Click **Finish** when the copying process is finished.

    You must now copy the template into the templates folder used by Excel. The default file path used is C:\Windows\ Application Data\Microsoft\Templates.

- Click the template called **2-1 Aztec Charter.xlt**.
- Open the **Edit** menu then click the **Copy** option to copy the template into the Windows clipboard.
- If necessary, scroll through the contents of the left pane of the window until you can see the **Windows** folder; click the plus (+) sign to the left of **Windows** in order to see a list of the folders it contains.

    The + sign becomes a - sign.

- Click the + sign to the left of the **Application Data** folder then click the + sign to the left of the **Microsoft** folder then finally click the **Templates** folder.

    By default, the templates are stored in this folder.

- Use the **Edit - Paste** command to copy the contents of the clipboard into the **Templates** folder.

    A dialog box appears while the copy is pasted in.

- When the copy is finished, click the ⊠ button on the **Explorer** window to close it.

    You can now put away the CD-ROM and start working on your MOUS exam preparation.

EXCEL 2000
Lesson 1.1: Overview

1 ■ Starting/leaving the Microsoft Excel 2000 application 12

2 ■ Using the Office Assistant 16

3 ■ Choosing the magnification of the workspace 17

4 ■ Undoing your last actions 18

5 ■ Redoing cancelled actions 18

Practice Exercise 1.1 20

EXCEL 2000
Lesson 1.1: Overview

1 ▪ Starting/leaving the Microsoft Excel 2000 application

Starting Excel 2000

- To start the Microsoft Excel 2000 application, click the **Start** button on the taskbar.
- With the mouse, point to the **Programs** option.
- Click the **Microsoft Excel** option.

  *As with all Windows applications, you work in an **application window** and, within that, a **document window**. An Excel document is called a workbook.*

The application window

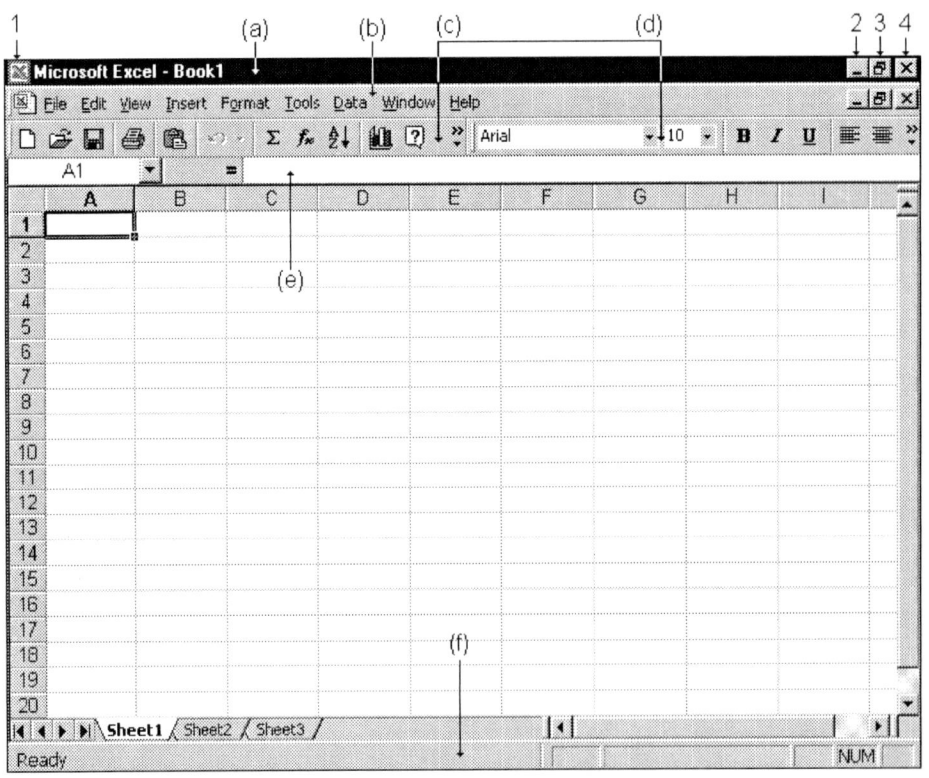

The **title bar** (a): on the left there is the button that opens the Excel **Control** (1) menu. Next to it, the name of the application (**Microsoft Excel**) and the name of the active workbook can be seen. On the right, there are the **Minimize** (2), **Maximize** or **Restore** (3) and **Close** (4) buttons.

The **menu bar** (b): this contains all the Excel menus. Each menu is made up of a list of the available options for the task at hand.

The **Standard** (c) and **Formatting toolbars** (d): these tools carry out common commands instantly and apply formatting.

The **formula bar** (e): this bar displays information on a given element (text, value or formula) so you can enter new data or edit existing ones.

The **status bar** (f): this bar gives information about a selected command or concerning the working environment. When **Ready** mode appears, you can start working.

EXCEL 2000
Lesson 1.1: Overview

The workbook window

When the workbook window is maximised to take up all the space in the application window, the workbook's **Control** menu button, as well as the **Minimize**, **Restore** and **Close** buttons are placed on the menu bar.

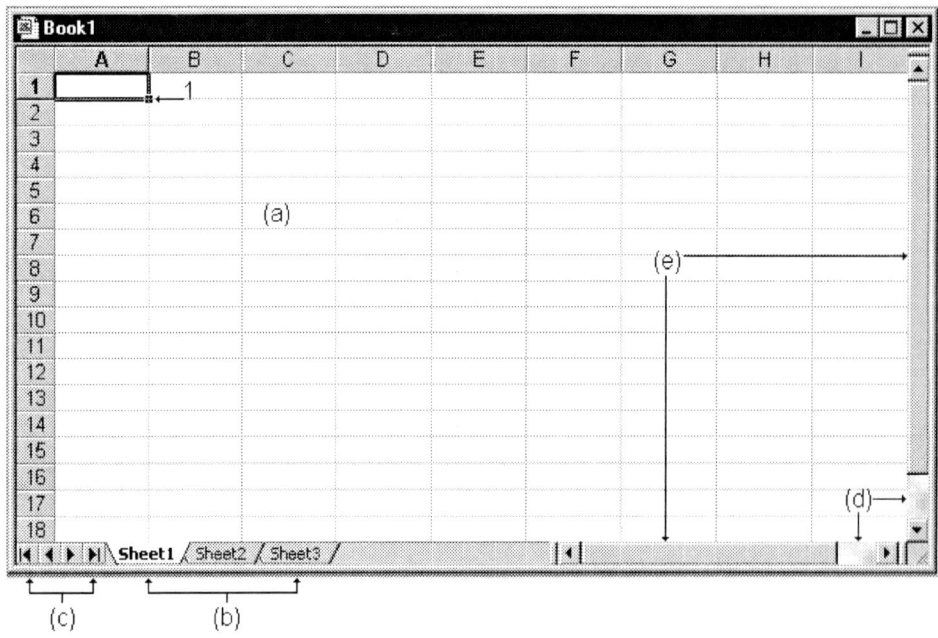

The **workspace** (a): this is the space in which you will be working.

In an Excel worksheet, each action is worked on a cell (or group of cells). Each **cell** is the intersection of a row with a column. Each cell's name is the association of the name of the column and the number of the row where it is located. For example, the cell located at the intersection of row 10 and column C is called C10 (this name is also known as the cell **reference**).

When you click a particular cell, it becomes the **active** cell. Its reference appears at the left of the formula bar.

In Excel 2000, you can use up to 256 columns and 65536 rows.

The black square in the bottom right corner of the active cell is called the **fill handle** (1).

Sheet tabs (b): a workbook is made up of several sheets. At the bottom of the workbook window, Excel displays the names of all the sheets on tabs, for easy identification. The name of the active sheet appears in bold type on a white tab.

The **tab scroll bar** (c): by default, each workbook contains three sheets.

The **scroll bars** (d): these are used to move up, down and across the active worksheet. The rectangles visible in the scroll bars (e) are called **scroll cursors** (or **scroll boxes**).

Leaving Excel 2000

- To leave the Microsoft Excel 2000 application, use the **File - Exit** command or click the ⊠ on the application window or press [Alt][F4].
- Save your modified documents, if required (the **Yes to All** option allows you to save all the open documents before leaving the application).

> A shortcut may have been created on the Windows Desktop; if this is the case, double-clicking the Microsoft Excel icon will start the application.

EXCEL 2000
Lesson 1.1: Overview

2 • Using the Office Assistant

- **Help - Show the Office Assistant**

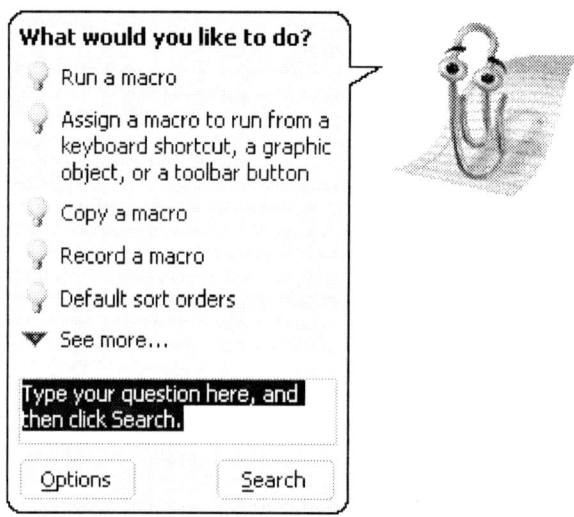

- Choose one of the proposed help topics or enter your query in everyday language (for example: **Calculating total repayments on a loan**) then click **Search**.

  Excel displays the help text corresponding to the chosen topic.

Changing the look of the Office Assistant

- Click the Assistant with the right mouse button then click **Choose Assistant**.
- Use the **Next** and/or **Back** buttons to see the other Assistants available.
- When you have chosen your Assistant, click **OK**.

MOUS
Excel 2000 Core

Hiding the Office Assistant

- Right-click the Office Assistant then click the **Hide** option.

Deactivating the Office Assistant

- Right-click the Assistant and click **Options**.
- Deactivate the **Use the Office Assistant** option on the **Options** page.

> *If the Office Assistant cannot provide the help you need, you can look for extra help on the Internet, either by clicking the **None of the above, look for more help on the Web** option among the Assistant's suggestions, or by using the **Office on the Web** option in the **Help** menu.*
>
> *When a light bulb appears next to the Assistant, this means it has some advice to offer you. Click the Assistant to read this tip.*

3 ▪ Choosing the magnification of the workspace

- **View - Zoom**

  The normal zoom level is 100%.

- Choose the **Magnification** that you require or activate the **Custom** option and enter your own zoom level.
- Click **OK**.

> *You can also use the* `100%` *list box to enter a value or choose one from the drop-down list.*

EXCEL 2000
Lesson 1.1: Overview

> The **View - Full Screen** option displays the worksheet over the entire screen.

4 • Undoing your last actions

- To undo the last action, use **Edit - Undo** or ⮌ or [Ctrl] **Z**.

- To undo several actions, click the arrow on the ⮌▼ tool button to open the list of the last actions made then click the earliest of the actions to undo (the one furthest down the list: this action plus all those that followed will be cancelled).

> In Excel 2000, you can undo up to 16 of the last actions. When certain actions cannot be undone, the **Edit** menu option becomes **Can't Undo**.

5 • Redoing cancelled actions

After having cancelled one, or several actions, you can redo them if you change your mind.

- To redo the last action undone, use the **Edit - Redo** command or ⮍ or [Ctrl] **Y**.

- To repeat several cancelled actions, click the arrow attached to the ⮍▼ tool to open the list of the last actions cancelled then click the earliest of the actions you want to redo (the one furthest down the list: this action and those following it will be restored).

This command is only available when one or more actions have previously been undone.

MOUS
Excel 2000 Core

Below, you can see **Practice Exercise** 1.1. This exercise is made up of 5 steps. If you do not know how to complete one of the steps, go back to the lesson to refer to the corresponding title. When you have finished, check your work by reading the **Solution** on the next page.

Steps that are likely to be tested on the exam are marked with a ⊞ symbol. It is however recommended that you follow the whole exercise in order to gain a complete understanding of the lesson.

☞ Practice Exercise 1.1

1. Start the Microsoft Excel 2000 application so you can see the workscreen.

⊞ 2. Show the Office Assistant then look at the help texts concerning how to save a workbook. Change the look of the Office Assistant then finish by hiding it.

⊞ 3. Modify the zoom level so you are viewing the workscreen at 80% magnification.

⊞ 4. Click in cell **A1** of the active worksheet then enter the text **MICROSOFT EXCEL 2000**. To this text, apply a bold then an italic type style.

   Use Excel's undo function to remove the bold and italic type.

⊞ 5. Use the redo function to reapply the bold type to your **MICROSOFT EXCEL 2000** text.

If you want to put what you have learnt into practice on a real document, you can work on summary exercise 1 for the OVERVIEW section, that you can find at the end of this book.

EXCEL 2000
Exercise 1.1: Overview

It is often possible to perform a task in several different ways, but here only the quickest solution is presented. Go back to the lesson to see the other techniques that can be used.

Solution to Exercise 1.1

1. To start the Microsoft Excel 2000 application, click the **Start** menu, point to the **Programs** option then click **Microsoft Excel**.

2. To show the Office Assistant, use the command **Help - Show the Office Assistant**.

   To see the available help about how to save a workbook, click the Office Assistant, type **save a workbook** in the text box and click the **Search** button.
   Click the **Save a workbook** topic, read the Help text then close the **Help** window by clicking the ⊠ button.

   To change the look of the Office Assistant, right-click it, click the **Choose Assistant** option then use the **Next** and/or **Back** buttons to choose a different Assistant. When your choice is made, click **OK** to confirm your choice.

   To hide the Office Assistant, right-click it then click the **Hide** option.

3. To change the working zoom to 80%, open the list on the `100%` tool, type **80** and confirm with ↵.

4. To remove the bold and italic type applied to the **MICROSOFT EXCEL 2000** text, open the list attached to the ↶ tool then click **Bold**.

5. To reapply the previously applied bold type to the **MICROSOFT EXCEL 2000**, text, click the ↷ tool.

WORKBOOKS AND WORKSHEETS
Lesson 2.1: Workbooks

1 ▪ Opening a workbook 22

2 ▪ Displaying an open workbook 23

3 ▪ Creating a new workbook 24

4 ▪ Creating a workbook based on a template 24

5 ▪ Saving a workbook 25

6 ▪ Saving a workbook under another name 26

7 ▪ Creating a folder 27

8 ▪ Saving a sheet/workbook as a Web page 28

9 ▪ Closing workbooks 30

10 ▪ Sending a worksheet/workbook by electronic mail 30

Practice Exercise 2.1 34

WORKBOOKS AND WORKSHEETS
Lesson 2.1: Workbooks

1 ▪ Opening a workbook

- **File - Open** or 📂 or `Ctrl` O

- To indicate where the document to be opened is located, click one of the buttons on the **Places Bar** (on the left side of the dialog box) or open the **Look in** drop-down list.

  The **History** button lets you view the 50 most recently used documents and/or folders. The **My Documents** button shows the contents of the **My Documents** folder. The **Desktop** shows the shortcuts installed on the Windows Desktop. The **Favorites** button opens the **Favorites** folder.

- Access the folder containing the document to be opened by double-clicking its icon.

- Click the ⬅ button to return to folders you have already used.

- To go to the folder above, click the ⬆ button.

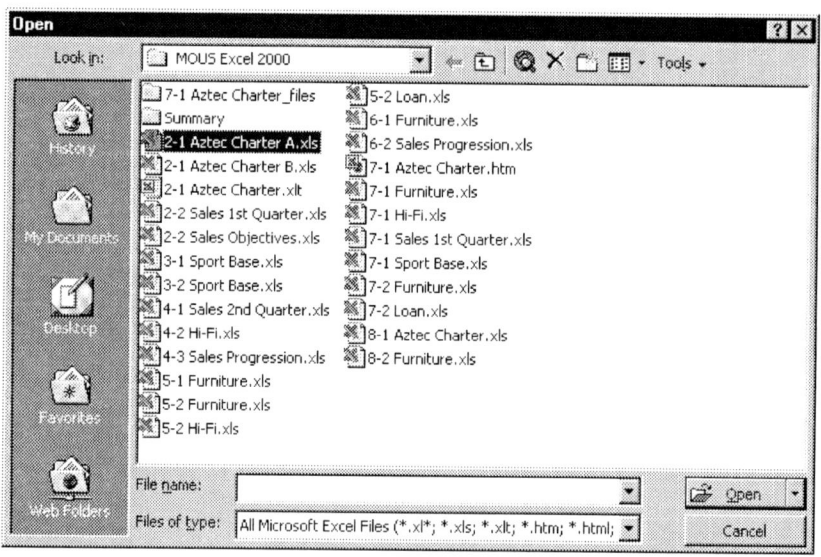

- Open the drop-down list on the [⊞▼] button then click one of the proposed options to change how the file list is displayed.

  *In **Detail** view, the name of each workbook appears in the first column and the list also displays the document's **Size**, its **Type** and the time and date of its last modification.*

- To display the properties of a selected workbook, open the drop-down list on the [⊞▼] button then click **Properties**.

- To see the contents of a given workbook, open the list on the [⊞▼] button then click the **Preview** option.

- To find, delete, rename or print one or more workbooks, click the **Tools** button then the option corresponding to your task.

- To open a workbook, select it then click **Open** or double-click its name.

  *The drop-down list on the **Open** button allows you to open a workbook in read-only mode, or to open a copy.*

2 ▪ Displaying an open workbook

- On the taskbar, click the button of the workbook you want to activate.

  You can also activate an open workbook using the **Window** menu.

  The open workbooks are listed in alphabetical order at the bottom of this menu. The active workbook is the one that is ticked.

  Click the workbook's name to activate it.

WORKBOOKS AND WORKSHEETS
Lesson 2.1: Workbooks

3 ▪ Creating a new workbook

- **File - New - OK** or ▭ or [Ctrl] **N**

    *A new workbook, called **BookX**, appears. This workbook is based on the default template.*

4 ▪ Creating a workbook based on a template

- **File - New**

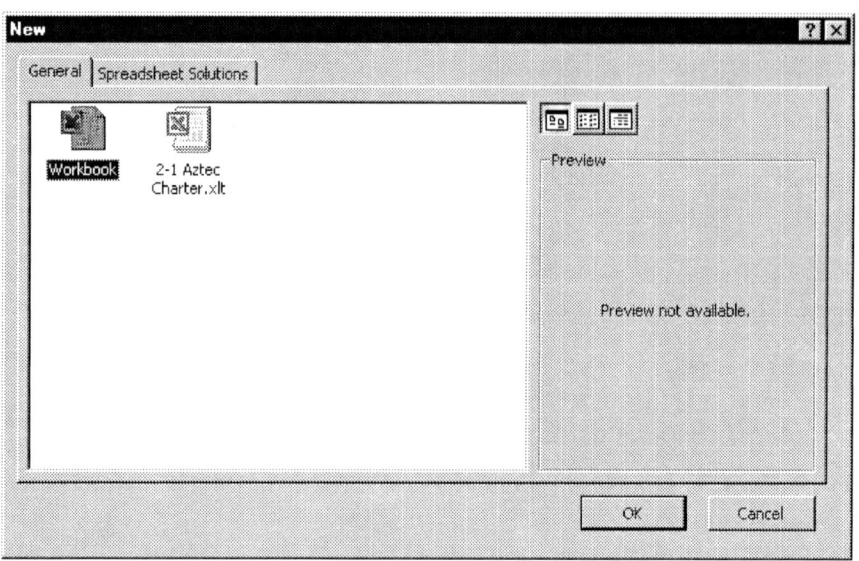

*The templates located in the **Templates** folder appear on the **General** page.*

- Double-click the template name.

    When you open a template, Excel copies its contents into a new workbook; this workbook takes the template name, followed by a number.

- Enter the information into the new workbook.

MOUS
Excel 2000 Core

- Save this new workbook as you would save any ordinary one.

5 ▪ Saving a workbook

A new workbook

- **File - Save** or 🖫 or **Ctrl** **S**
- Using the **Save in** drop-down, choose the drive in which you want to save the workbook; you can also use one of the icons on the **Places Bar.**
- Go into the folder where you want to save the workbook by double-clicking the folder icon.
- Double-click the **File name** text box then enter the name you want to give to the workbook: you can use up to 255 characters, including spaces.

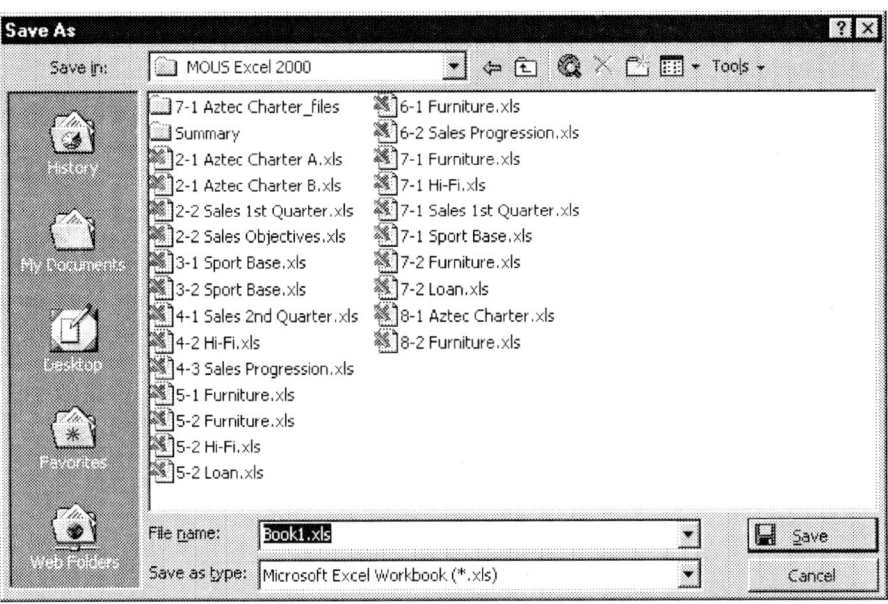

WORKBOOKS AND WORKSHEETS
Lesson 2.1: Workbooks

- Click the **Save** button.

    The workbook name appears on the title bar: Excel workbooks take an .xls extension (which may not necessarily be visible).

    An existing workbook

- **File - Save** or or `Ctrl` **S**

    > It is possible to save your documents automatically, by installing the **AutoSave** add-in (use the **Tools - Add-Ins** command). Once you have installed the add-in, the **AutoSave** option becomes available in the **Tools** menu.

    > If you are closing a workbook or leaving Excel, you may want to click the cell that should be active the next time the document is opened, before you save it.

6 ▪ Saving a workbook under another name

- Open the workbook that you want to duplicate by using **File - Open** or ⮕ or `Ctrl` **O**.
- Make any changes required in the workbook.
- **File - Save As**

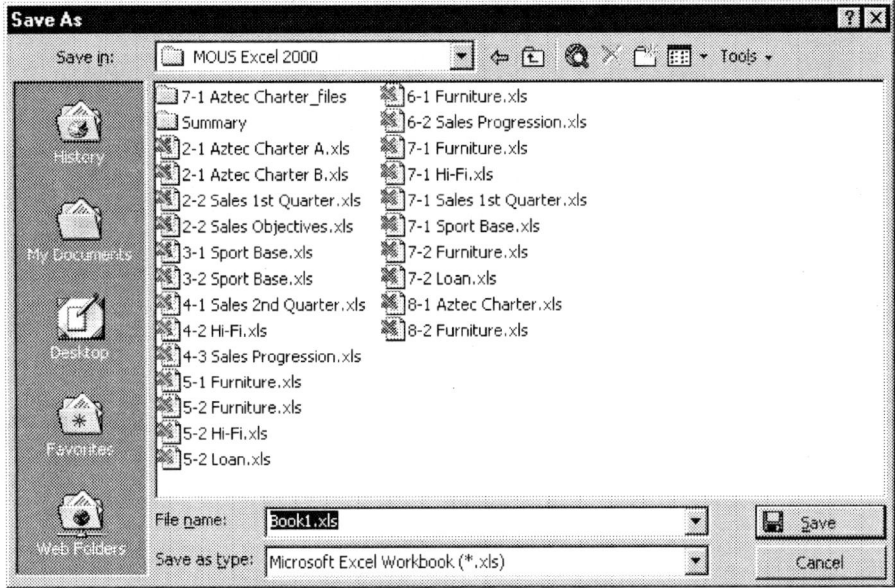

- Select the drive, then the folder in which the workbook should be saved.
- In the **Save as type** list, select, if necessary, the format in which the file should be saved.
- Enter a new file name in the **File name** text box.
- Click the **Save** button.

The changes made to the workbook are only saved in the copy and it is this copy that now appears on the screen.

7 - Creating a folder

It is possible that when you save a workbook, the folder in which you want to save it may not exist. You can create a new folder directly from Excel.

- **File - Save** or **File - Save As**

*You can also create a new folder from the Open dialog box (**File - Open**).*

WORKBOOKS AND WORKSHEETS
Lesson 2.1: Workbooks

- Select the drive then the folder in which you wish to create a new folder.
- Click the ▢ tool.

The path to and the name of the folder in which the new folder will be created appear above the **Name** text box.

- Enter the **Name** for the folder in the corresponding box.
- Click **OK**.
- Close the dialog box by clicking the ▢ button or save the active workbook by clicking the **Save** button.

8 ▪ Saving a sheet/workbook as a Web page

This technique allows you to save a worksheet or workbook in HTML format in order to make it available on the Internet or an intranet network. The information contained the page can be consulted by network users but cannot be modified.

- Create or open the workbook you want to transform into a Web page.
- **File - Save as Web Page**
- Open the **Save in** list and select the folder where you want to save the Web page and its components.
- Use the **Web Options** in the **Tools** menu to change the parameters of the Web page currently being created.

- Choose to either save the **Entire Workbook** or just a **Selection** (a sheet or cell range).
- Click the **Change Title** button to enter the text that will be displayed on the browser title bar when the Web page is opened.

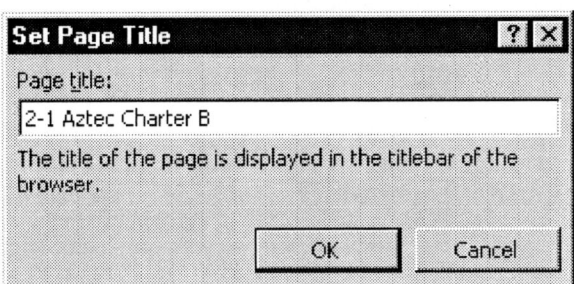

- Click **OK**.
- If necessary, modify the proposed **File name**.

  It is preferable to avoid spaces and accents, which are not always correctly interpreted by Web servers.

- Choose **Web Page (*.htm ; *.html)** format in the **Save as type** box.
- Click **Save**.

  The Web page in htm format appears and the original file closes automatically. In addition to the Web page (htm format) Excel creates a folder containing the various components of the Web page (these are called the supporting files). For example:

Name	Size	Type	Modified
2-1 Aztec Charter B_files		File Folder	18/01/00 15:30
2-1 Aztec Charter B.htm	13KB	HTML Document	18/01/00 15:30

The Web page and this folder are indissociable.

WORKBOOKS AND WORKSHEETS
Lesson 2.1: Workbooks

9 ▪ Closing workbooks

A single workbook

- **File - Close** or click the ⊠ button on the workbook window or `Ctrl` `F4` or `Ctrl` **W**
- When prompted, save the changes made to the workbook, if required.

All open workbooks

- Open the **File** menu while holding down the `Shift` key.

  *The option normally called **Close** is transformed into **Close All**.*

- Click the **Close All** option.
- As is necessary, choose whether or not to save any modified workbooks (the **Yes to All** option saves all the workbooks).

10 ▪ Sending a worksheet/workbook by electronic mail

If you have e-mail software installed on your computer, you can send a sheet or a workbook to a third party directly from Excel.

Sending a worksheet as the body of a message

This technique allows the recipient to read the data you send, even if the Excel application is not installed on his/her computer.

- Open the workbook then activate the sheet you want to send.
- **File - Send To - Mail Recipient** or

  *The first time you use this command, a dialog box appears and asks whether you wish to **Send the entire workbook as an attachment** or **Send the current sheet as the message body**. Choose the second option.*

MOUS
Excel 2000 Core

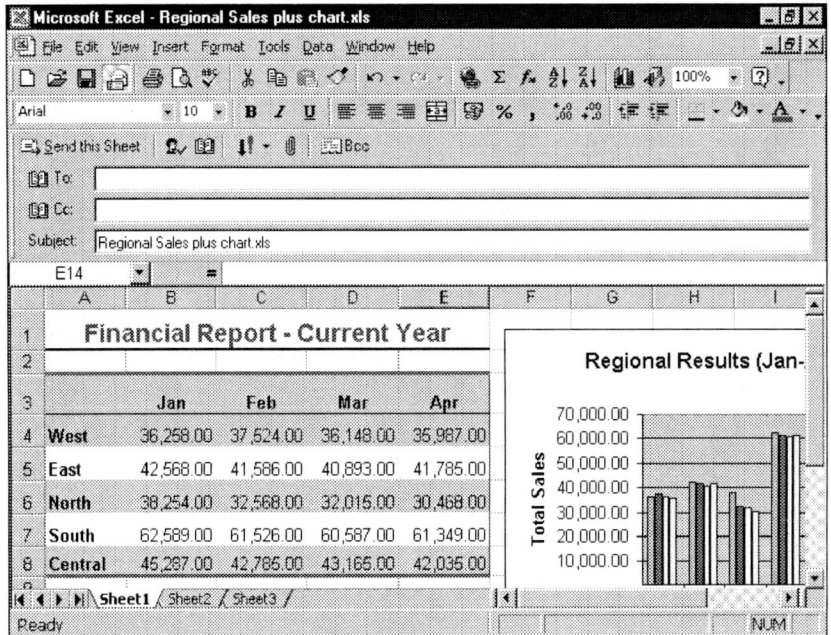

This screen may differ depending on the e-mail software used by default.

- In the **To** box, type in the e-mail address(es) of the recipient(s), separating each name with a semi-colon, or click the to choose the address(es) from the address book.

- In the **Cc** box, indicate any addresses to which you want to send a carbon copy of the message.

- In the **Subject** box, change the message title if necessary; by default the workbook name appears in this box.

- Click the **Send this Sheet** button.

  A copy of the active worksheet is sent to the mail recipient. This sheet makes up the body of the message.

  To close the e-mail window without sending the message, click the button on the **Standard** toolbar again.

31

WORKBOOKS AND WORKSHEETS
Lesson 2.1: Workbooks

Sending a workbook as an attached file

Using this method implies that the recipient has Excel installed on his/her computer.

- Open the workbook you want to send, or create it if it does not already exist.

Only a whole workbook and not just a part of it can be sent.

- **File - Send To - Mail Recipient (as Attachment)**

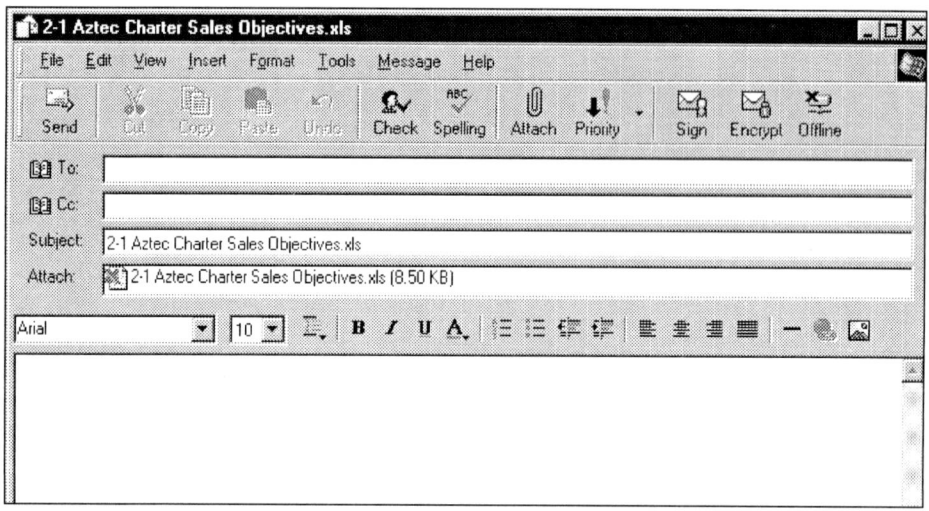

The new message window of your e-mail software (Outlook Express in this example) appears. Depending on the software used, the attachment may appear as an icon in the bottom of the window, or, as here, as an icon on the header bar. Depending on the file format used (rich or plain text), the bottom part of this window may be divided into one or two panes.

- In the **To** box, enter the address(es) of the message recipient(s), separating each name with a semi-colon. You can also click the [To:] button to select the address(es) from the address book.

- In the **Cc** box, indicate, if necessary, any addresses to which you want to send a carbon copy.

- In the **Subject** box, enter or modify the message subject, as required.
- To enter a comment with the attachment, click the space provided for the body of the message (the interior of the window) and type in your message.

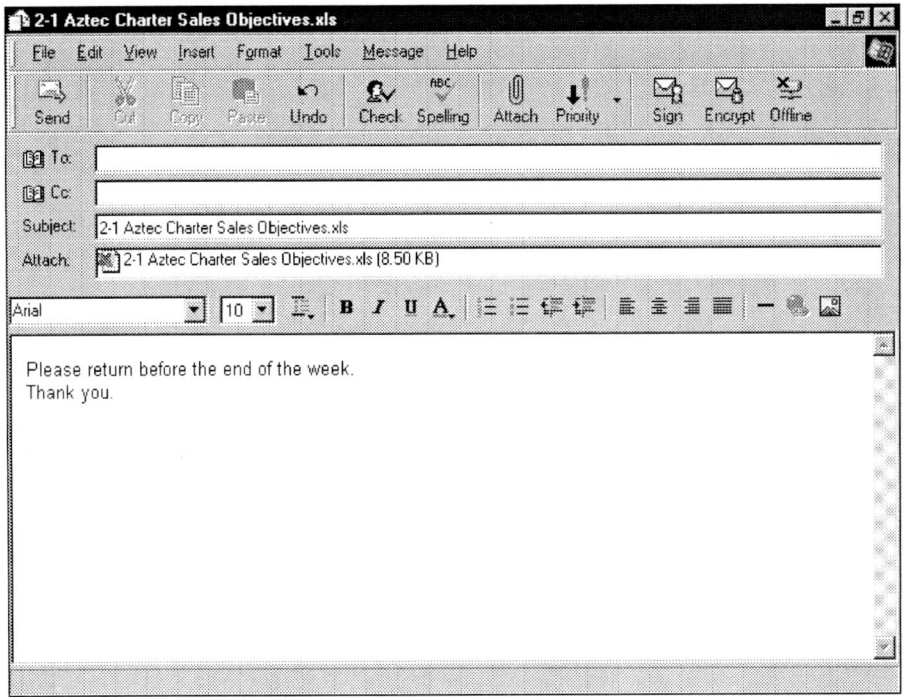

- Click the **Send** button.
- To open or change an attachment, the recipient must open the message then double-click the attachment's icon. Opening this file will start the Excel application automatically.

> To close the e-mail window without sending the message, click the ⊠ button. Excel prompts you to save the document. If you click **Yes**, the message will be saved in the **Drafts** folder, on in the **Inbox**, depending on your e-mail software. You can then send it at a later time if you wish.

WORKBOOKS AND WORKSHEETS
Exercise 2.1: Workbooks

Below, you can see **Practice Exercise** 2.1. This exercise is made up of 10 steps. If you do not know how to complete one of the steps, go back to the lesson to refer to the corresponding title. When you have finished, check your work by reading the **Solution** on the next page.

Steps that are likely to be tested on the exam are marked with a 🔲 symbol. It is however recommended that you follow the whole exercise in order to gain a complete understanding of the lesson.

☞ Practice Exercise 2.1

1. Open the **2-1 Aztec Charter A.xls** and **2-1 Aztec Charter B.xls** workbooks located in the **MOUS Excel 2000** folder.

2. Display the **2-1 Aztec Charter A.xls** workbook on the screen.

3. Create a new workbook.

4. Create a new workbook based on the **2-1 Aztec Charter.xlt** template.

5. Save the new workbook based on the **2-1 Aztec Charter.xlt** template in the **MOUS Excel 2000** folder. You can call this workbook **2-1 Aztec Charter C.xls**.

6. In the **MOUS Excel 2000** folder, save the **2-1 Aztec Charter C.xls** workbook under the name **2-1 Aztec Charter Sales Objectives**.

7. In the **MOUS Excel 2000** folder, create a new folder called **Web Pages**.

8. Display the **2-1 Aztec Charter B.xls** workbook on the screen then save it as a Web page in the **Web Pages** folder. You do not have to change the document name.

9. Close all the open workbooks in Microsoft Excel 2000.

10. Open the **2-1 Aztec Charter Sales Objectives.xls** workbook then use e-mail to send it as an attached file to the recipient of your choice. Add the following text to the message:

**Please return before the end of the week.
Thank you.**

If you want to put what you have learnt into practice on a real document, you can work on summary exercise 2 for the WORKBOOKS AND WORKSHEETS section, that you can find at the end of this book.

WORKBOOKS AND WORKSHEETS
Exercise 2.1: Workbooks

It is often possible to perform a task in several different ways, but here only the quickest solution is presented. Go back to the lesson to see the other techniques that can be used.

Solution to Exercise 2.1

1. To open the **2-1 Aztec Charter A.xls** and **2-1 Aztec Charter B.xls** workbooks, located in the **MOUS Excel 2000** folder, click the tool, open the **Look in** drop-down list then select the disk drive where you copied the documents from the CD-ROM provided with this book.

    Double-click the **MOUS Excel 2000** folder, click the **2-1 Aztec Charter A.xls** file then hold down the Ctrl key and click the **2-1 Aztec Charter B.xls**.

    Click the **Open** button.

2. To display the **2-1 Aztec Charter A.xls** workbook on the screen, click the button on the taskbar that corresponds to the **2-1 Aztec Charter A.xls** workbook.

3. To create a new workbook, click the tool.

4. To create a new workbook based on the **2-1 Aztec Charter** template, use the **File - New** command then on the **General** page, double-click the **2-1 Aztec Charter.xlt** icon.

MOUS
Excel 2000 Core

5. To save the new workbook created from the **2-1 Aztec Charter** template, click the ▣ tool.

    Open the **Save in** drop-down list, select the disk drive in which the **MOUS Excel 2000** folder is located then double-click the **MOUS Excel 2000** folder to open it.

    Enter **2-1 Aztec Charter C** in the **File name** text box. Click the **Save** button.

6. To save the **2-1 Aztec Charter C.xls** workbook in the **MOUS Excel 2000** folder under the name of **2-1 Aztec Charter Sales Objectives**, use the **File - Save As** command.

    Open the **Save in** drop-down list, selec the drive in which the **MOUS Excel 2000** folder is stored and double-click the folder icon.

    Leave **Microsoft Excel Workbook (*.xls)** in the **Save as type** box then enter **2-1 Aztec Charter Sales Objectives** as the **File name**. Finish by clicking the **Save** button.

7. To create a new folder within the **MOUS Excel 2000** folder called **Web Pages**, use the **File - Save As** command.

    Open the **Save in** drop-down list, select the drive where the **MOUS Excel 2000** folder is located and double-click its icon.

    Click the ▣ tool, enter **Web Pages** then click **OK**.

    Close the dialog box by clicking the ▣ button.

8. To save the **2-1 Aztec Charter B.xls** workbook as a Web page, start by displaying it: click the **2-1 Aztec Charter B.xls** button on the taskbar.

    Choose the **File - Save as Web Page** command.

    Select the drive containing the **MOUS Excel 2000** folder and double-click its icon, then double-click the **Web Pages** folder.

WORKBOOKS AND WORKSHEETS
Exercise 2.1: Workbooks

Leave the **Entire Workbook** option active and do not change the **File name**. Click the **Save** button.

9. To close all the workbooks currently open in Microsoft Excel, hold down the [Shift] key and use the **File - Close All** command.

10. To send the **2-1 Aztec Charter Sales Objectives** workbook as an attached file in an e-mail to a given recipient, open the **2-1 Aztec Charter Sales Objectives** workbook, located in the **MOUS Excel 2000** folder.

Use the **File - Send To - Mail Recipient (as Attachment)** command.

Enter the recipient's address in the **To** box. Click inside the message window and type **Please return before the end of the week.**, press ⏎ then type **Thank you**.

Click the **Send** button.

WORKBOOKS AND WORKSHEETS
Lesson 2.2: Worksheets

1. Moving around within a worksheet.. 40

2. Moving from one sheet to another... 41

3. Naming a sheet 42

4. Moving a sheet within a workbook 42

5. Copying a sheet into a workbook.. 42

6. Moving/copying a sheet from one workbook to another................................ 43

7. Deleting sheets 44

8. Inserting sheets 44

9. Consolidating worksheets.. 45

10. Creating a link between sheets 46

Practice Exercise 2.2 48

WORKBOOKS AND WORKSHEETS
Lesson 2.2: Worksheets

1 ▪ Moving around in a worksheet

You can choose between several techniques, depending on which tool you want to use: the mouse or the keyboard.

▪ Use the scroll bars to move the sheet until you see the cell you want to activate:

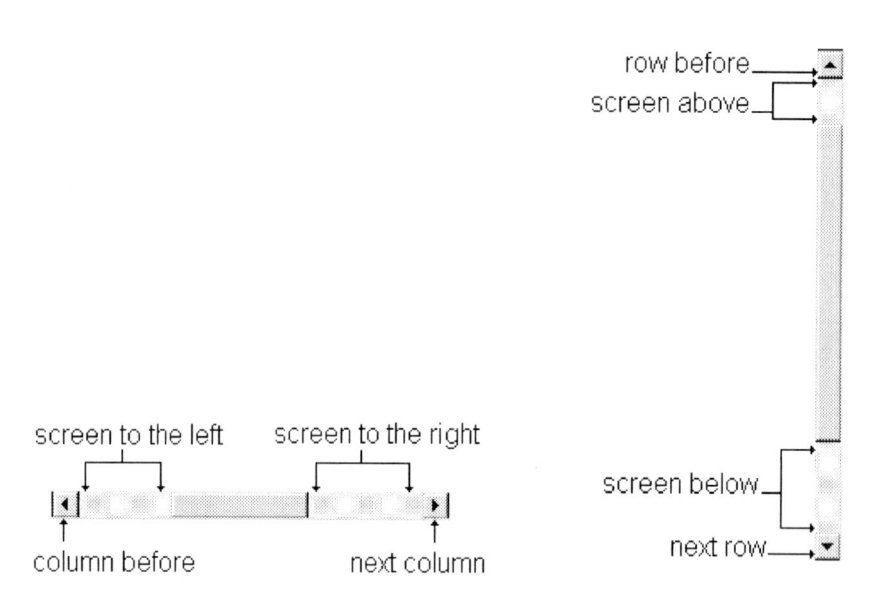

row before
screen above

screen to the left   screen to the right

column before   next column

screen below
next row

When you drag the scroll cursor, a ScreenTip appears, showing the row number or column letter currently reached.

▪ Use the keyboard in the following way:

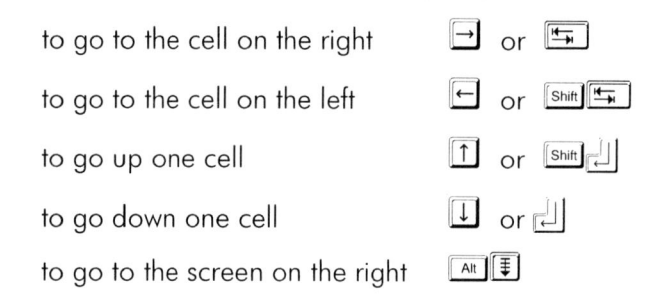

to go to the cell on the right	→	or [Tab]
to go to the cell on the left	←	or Shift [Tab]
to go up one cell	↑	or Shift ↵
to go down one cell	↓	or ↵
to go to the screen on the right	Alt PgDn	

MOUS
Excel 2000 Core

to go to the screen on the left   `Alt` `PgUp`

to go up one screen   `PgUp`

to go down one screen   `PgDn`

column A of the active row   `Home`

cell A1   `Ctrl` `Home`

- To go to a specific cell, double-click the name box, type in the cell reference then enter.

2 • Moving from one sheet to another

At the bottom of each worksheet, Excel shows the tabs of all the sheets it contains so you can identify them. The name of the active sheet appears in bold type on a white tab.

- Using the tab scroll buttons, scroll the sheets tabs until you can see the one where you want to go.

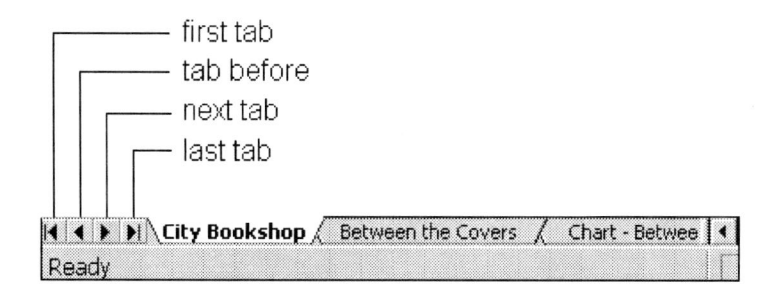

          first tab
          tab before
          next tab
          last tab

- Click the tab of the sheet that you want to see.

     You can also use the `Ctrl` `PgDn` *and* `Ctrl` `PgUp` *keys to go to the next sheet and the previous sheet, respectively.*

41

WORKBOOKS AND WORKSHEETS
Lesson 2.2: Worksheets

3 • Naming a sheet

This name appears on the sheet tab.

- Double-click the tab of the sheet you want to rename.
- Type the new name over the sheet's previous name.

This name cannot contain more than 31 characters (including spaces). It should not be placed between brackets, nor contain these characters: colon (:), slash (/), backslash (\), question mark (?) or asterisk (*).

- Press ⏎ to confirm.

4 • Moving a sheet within a workbook

- Click the tab you want to move.
- Drag this tab into its new position.

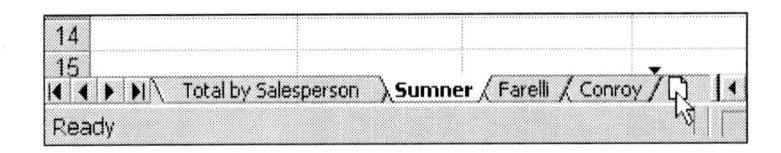

- When you are satisfied with the sheet's position, you can release the mouse button.

5 • Copying a sheet in a workbook

- Click the tab of the sheet you want to copy.
- While holding down the Ctrl key, drag to the position in which you want to place the copy of the sheet.
- When you are satisfied with the sheet's position, release the mouse button.

MOUS
Excel 2000 Core

B6 ▪ Moving/copying a sheet from one workbook to another

- Open the workbook containing the sheet you wish to transfer and the destination workbook.
- Go into the sheet you want to move/copy.
- **Edit - Move or Copy Sheet**
- Open the list called **To book** and click the name of the destination workbook.
- In the **Before sheet** list box, select the sheet in the destination workbook in front of which you want to insert the other sheet.
- Activate, if necessary, the **Create a copy** option.

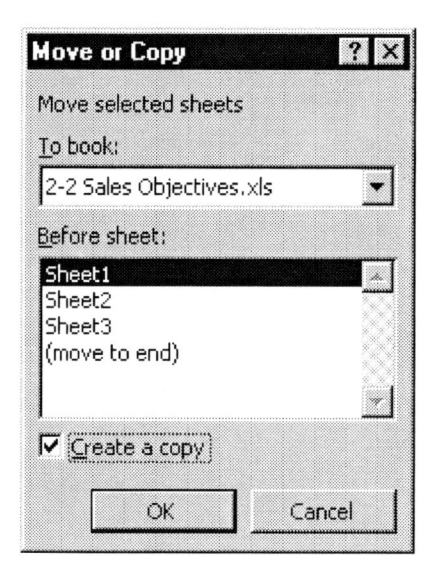

- Click **OK**.

  The destination workbook becomes the active workbook.

WORKBOOKS AND WORKSHEETS
Lesson 2.2: Worksheets

7 • Deleting sheets

- Select the sheets you wish to delete. If they are adjacent, click the first tab, hold down the [Shift] key and click the last; if they are non-adjacent, hold down [Ctrl] and click each sheet tab concerned.
- **Edit - Delete Sheet**

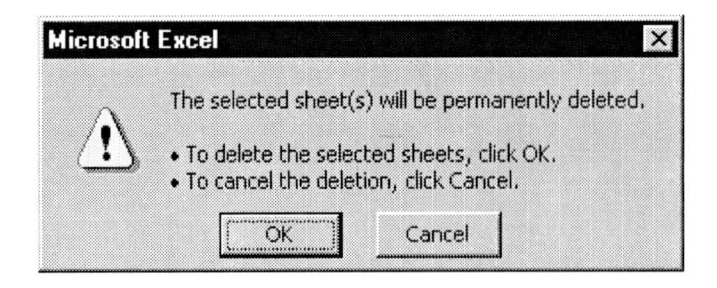

If the Office Assistant is visible, this confirmation prompt will appear in a pale yellow ScreenTip.

- Confirm your request by clicking **OK**.

8 • Inserting sheets

- Decide where you want to insert the new sheet and select the sheet that will come after it.
- To insert several sheets at once, hold down the [Shift] key and select as many sheet tabs as you want to insert new sheets.
- **Insert - Worksheet**

9 ▪ Consolidating worksheets

This technique allows you to make calculations (an addition for example) using values contained in several tables.

- Activate the first destination cell of the consolidation.
- **Data - Consolidate**
- From the **Function** list, choose the calculation you want to perform.
- Go into the **Reference** box.
- For each sheet to be consolidated:

    - click the [icon] button to minimise the dialog box,

    - activate the worksheet then select the cells concerned,

    - click the [icon] button to restore the dialog box,

    - click the **Add** button.
- If you have included data labels in your selection, indicate where they are located by checking one of the boxes under **Use labels in**.
- If you wish to create a permanent link between the source sheets and the destination sheet, activate the **Create links to source data** check box.

WORKBOOKS AND WORKSHEETS
Lesson 2.2: Worksheets

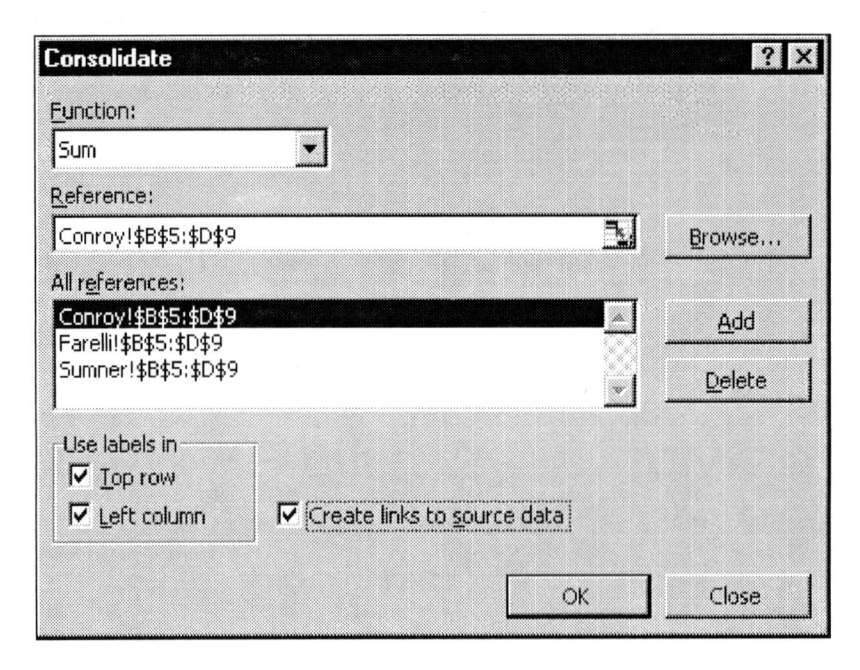

- Click **OK**.

    After a few seconds the results of the consolidation appear. If you choose to create a link, Excel also produces an outline of the table.

Creating a link between sheets

This technique is used to insert in a worksheet a formula referring to cells in another sheet.

- Select the destination cell.
- Type =
- Enter the formula, selecting the cells in the sheet(s) concerned. To go to a cell located in another sheet, click the sheet tab then the cell.

MOUS
Excel 2000 Core

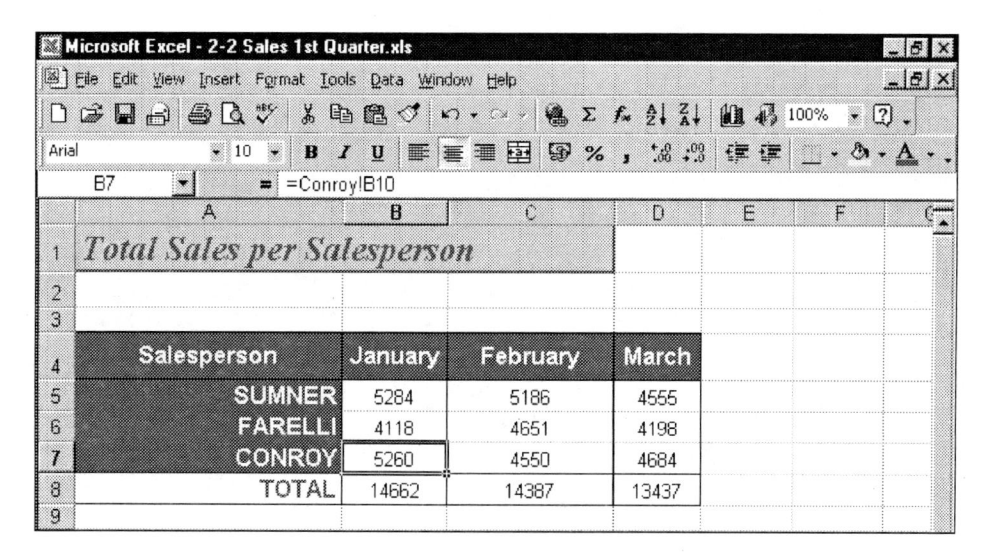

	A	B	C	D	E	F
1	*Total Sales per Salesperson*					
2						
3						
4	Salesperson	January	February	March		
5	SUMNER	5284	5186	4555		
6	FARELLI	4118	4651	4198		
7	CONROY	5260	4550	4684		
8	TOTAL	14662	14387	13437		
9						

B7 = =Conroy!B10

In the formula, the cell name is preceded by the name of the source worksheet. Cell B7 contains a formula that displays the value of cell B10 in the **Conroy** worksheet.

- Confirm with ⏎.

WORKBOOKS AND WORKSHEETS
Exercise 2.2: Worksheets

Below you can see **Practice Exercise** 2.2. This exercise is made up of 10 steps. If you do not know how to complete one of the steps, go back to the lesson to refer to the corresponding task. When you have finished, check your work by reading the **Solution** on the next page.

Steps that are likely to be tested on the exam are marked with a 🄱 symbol. It is however recommended that you follow the whole exercise in order to gain a complete understanding of the lesson.

☞ Practice Exercise 2.2 ✓

In order to complete exercise 2.2, you should open the **2-2 Sales 1st Quarter.xls** workbook located in the **MOUS Excel 2000** folder

1. Display column **F** of the active worksheet on the screen, then return to cell **A1**.

🄱 2. Display on the screen the contents of **Sheet2**.

🄱 3. Name **Sheet1** as **Sumner**, Sheet2 as Farelli, and **Sheet3** as **Conroy**.

🄱 4. Move the **Total by Salesperson** sheet after the **Conroy** sheet.

🄱 5. Insert a copy of the **Total by Salesperson** sheet in front of the **Sumner** sheet.

🄱 6. Place a copy of the **Sumner** sheet in front of the **Sheet1** sheet in the **2-2 Sales Objectives** workbook, located in the **MOUS Excel 2000** folder.

   Close the **2-2 Sales Objectives.xls** workbook, saving your changes when prompted.

7. Delete the first worksheet in the workbook, called **Total by Salesperson (2)**.

8. Insert a worksheet between the **Conroy** and **Total by Salesperson** sheets and call it **Consolidation**.

9. Create a new table in the **Consolidation** sheet, in order to consolidate the data contained in the **Sumner**, **Farelli** and **Conroy** sheets. This new table should contain the **Sum** of the three tables **Sumner**, **Farelli** and **Conroy** and should be linked to the data in these three source tables.

10. Complete the table in the **Total by Salesperson** sheet by inserting the figures for the salesperson called **Conroy** for **January** from the data contained in the **Conroy** worksheet.

If you want to put what you have learnt into practice on a real document, you can work on summary exercise 2 for the WORKBOOKS AND WORKSHEETS section that you can find at the end of this book.

WORKBOOKS AND WORKSHEETS
Exercise 2.2: Worksheets

It is often possible to perform a task in several different ways, but here only the quickest solution is presented. Go back to the lesson to see the other techniques that can be used.

Solution to Exercise 2.2

1. To display column **F** of the active worksheet on the screen, press [Alt][↓]. To go back to cell **A1**, press [Ctrl][↖].

2. To display the contents of **Sheet2** on the screen, click the **Sheet2** tab.

3. To rename the **Sheet1** sheet as **Sumner** double-click the **Sheet1** tab, type **Sumner** then confirm by pressing [↵].

   To rename the **Sheet2** sheet as **Farelli**, double-click the **Sheet2** tab, type **Farelli** then confirm by pressing [↵].

   To rename the **Sheet3** sheet as **Conroy**, double-click the **Sheet3** tab then type **Conroy** and confirm by pressing [↵].

4. To move the **Total by Salesperson** sheet to the right of the **Conroy** sheet, click the **Total by Salesperson** tab and drag it in position to the right of the **Conroy** tab.

5. To make a copy of the **Total by Salesperson** sheet and move it in front of the **Sumner** sheet, click the **Total by Salesperson** tab then hold down the [Ctrl] key and drag this tab in front of the **Sumner** tab.

MOUS
Excel 2000 Core

6. To make a copy of the **Sumner** sheet and place that copy in front of the **Sheet1** sheet in the **2-2 Sales Objectives.xls** workbook, first open the **2-2 Sales Objectives.xls** workbook in the **MOUS Excel 2000** folder then return the **2-2 Sales 1st Quarter.xls** workbook to the screen.

   Click the tab of the **Sumner** sheet then use the **Edit - Move or Copy Sheet** command.
   Open the **To book** list and select the **2-2 Sales Objectives.xls** workbook.
   In the **Before sheet** text box, leave **Sheet1** selected.
   Activate the **Create a copy** option then click **OK**.

   Close the **2-2 Sales Objectives.xls** workbook by click the ⊠ button on the workbook window then click the **Yes** button when prompted to save the changes made.

7. To delete the first worksheet in the workbook, called **Total by Salesperson (2)**, click the **Total by Salesperson (2)** tab then use the **Edit - Delete Sheet** command.
   Click **OK** to confirm this deletion.

8. To insert a worksheet between the **Conroy** and **Total by Salesperson** sheets, click the **Total by Salesperson** tab and use the **Insert - Worksheet** command.

   To name the sheet you have just inserted, double-click its tab, type **Consolidation** then confirm by pressing ⏎.

WORKBOOKS AND WORKSHEETS
Exercise 2.2: Worksheets

9. To create a table in the **Consolidation** sheet, in order to consolidate the data contained in the tables on the **Sumner**, **Farelli** and **Conroy** sheets, click in the **Consolidation** worksheet then use the **Data - Consolidate** command.
Select **Sum** in the **Function** list.

Click the ▦ button on the **Reference** text box then click the **Sumner** tab. Drag from cell **A4** to cell **D10**, click the ▦ button again then press the **Add** button.

Click the ▦ button on the **Reference** text box then click the **Farelli** tab. Click the ▦ button again then click **Add**.

Click the ▦ button on the **Reference** text box then click the **Conroy** tab. Click the ▦ button again then click **Add**.

Activate the **Top row**, **Left column** and **Create links to source data** options then click **OK**.

10. To complete the table on the **Total by Salesperson** sheet by adding the figures for **Conroy** for the month of January, click the **Total by Salesperson** tab.
Click cell **B7** and type =
Click the **Conroy** tab then click cell **B10** and confirm by pressing ↵.

ROWS, COLUMNS AND CELLS
Lesson 3.1: Rows/Columns

1 ≫ Selecting rows/columns 54

2 ≫ Inserting rows/columns 54

3 ≫ Deleting rows/columns 55

4 ≫ Hiding rows/columns 56

5 ≫ Showing hidden rows/columns 57

6 ≫ Freezing/unfreezing rows and/or columns 58

7 ≫ Changing column width/row height 59

8 ≫ Adjusting columns/rows to fit contents 60

Practice Exercise 3.1 61

ROWS, COLUMNS AND CELLS
Lesson 3.1: Rows/Columns

1 ▪ Selecting rows/columns

- Use one of the following techniques:

	Row	Column
🖱	click the row number to select it.	click the column letter to select it.
⌨	activate a cell in the required row and press [Shift][Space].	activate a cell in the required column and press [Ctrl][Space].

When a row (or column) is selected, its number (or letter) appears in a dark colour.

To select several adjacent rows or columns, use the mouse to drag over the row or column headings. If the rows or columns are not adjacent, hold down the [Ctrl] key while you select each row or column.

2 ▪ Inserting rows/columns

- 🖱 Decide where you want to insert the new row (or column) and select the row (or column) under (or right of) that position.

- Point to the fill handle.

  Make sure the mouse pointer has become a fine black cross.

- Hold down [Shift] and without releasing the key, drag the fill handle over the same number of rows (or columns) as you want to insert new ones.

  When inserting rows you must drag downwards, not upwards, and for columns, drag towards the right (and not left).

- Release first the mouse button then the [Shift] key.

  As you drag, you notice that you are actually dragging a grey bar.

  > *With this technique, it is not possible to insert rows before row 1 or columns before column A.*

- Decide where you want to insert the new row/column and select the row/column below/right of that position.

  To insert several rows or columns, select as many rows/columns as you want to insert new ones.

- **Insert - Rows** or **Columns**

▪ Deleting rows/columns

- Select the rows (or columns) you want to delete.
- Point to the fill handle (the pointer should become a fine black cross).
- Press the [Shift] key and without letting it go, drag upwards over the rows (or left over the columns) until you have dragged over as many rows or columns as you wish to delete.

  When you drag, the selected areas change colour.

- Release first the mouse then the [Shift] key.

  > *The **Delete** command in the **Edit** menu will also delete the selected row(s) or column(s).*

  > *You can also delete rows or columns by selecting them and pressing [Ctrl] -.*

ROWS, COLUMNS AND CELLS
Lesson 3.1: Rows/Columns

4 ▪ Hiding rows/columns

- Select the rows or columns that you want to hide. If hiding only one row or column, simply click a cell inside it.

- In the row or column heading, point to the horizontal line under the row number or the vertical line to the right of the column heading.

  You notice that the pointer now looks like this: ↔

- For columns drag left, or for rows drag up, until the row height or column width shown in the ScreenTip that appears equals **0**.

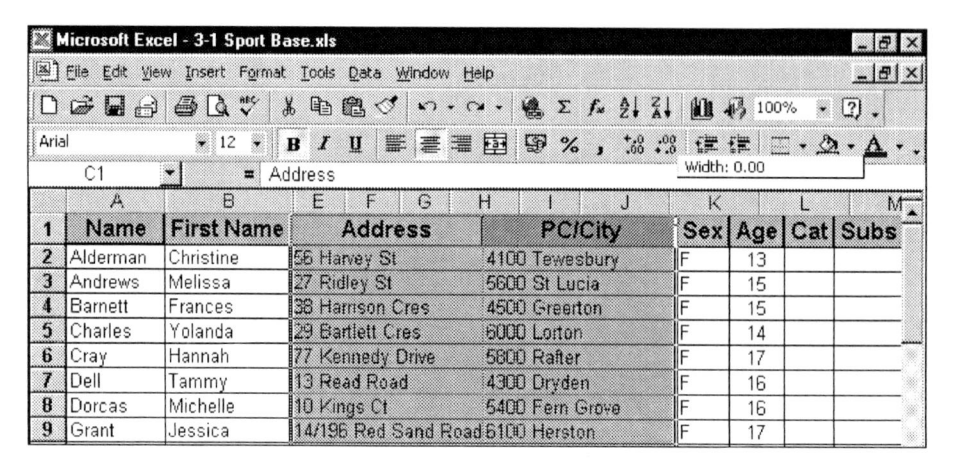

- Release the mouse button.

  You can no longer see the headings of rows/columns that have been hidden.

- Select the rows or columns that you want to hide. If only one row or column is concerned, click any cell inside it.
- **Format - Row** or **Column** or right-click one of the selected row or column headings.
- Click the **Hide** option.

▪ Showing hidden rows/columns

This method allows you to display one hidden row or column at a time.

- In the row or column heading, point to the horizontal line beneath the row number or the vertical line to the right of the column letter then move the pointer slightly down (row) or right (column) until the pointer changes shape and becomes: ↔.

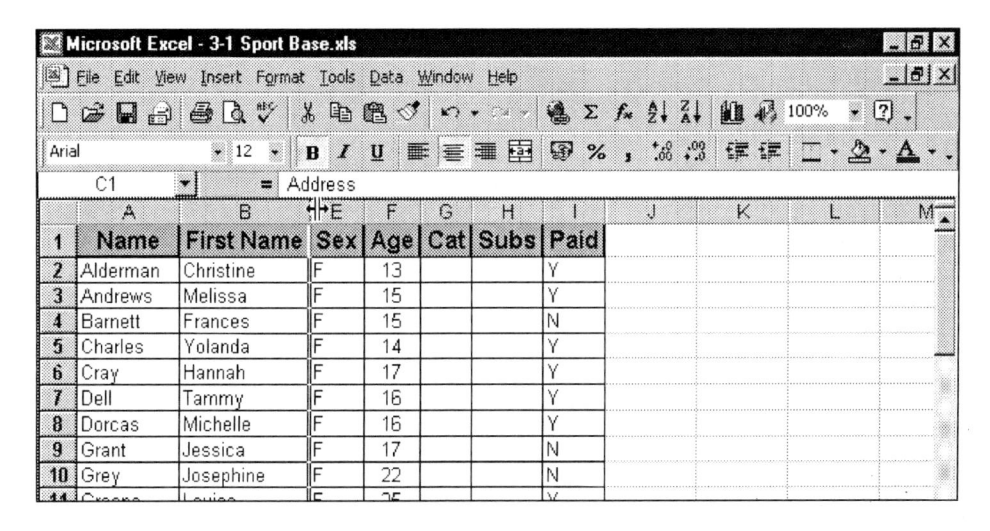

- Drag right to show the hidden column, or down to show the hidden row.
- Release the mouse button.

*This method is useful when you want to unhide column **A** and/or row **1**.*

ROWS, COLUMNS AND CELLS
Lesson 3.1: Rows/Columns

- To show hidden columns, select the columns to the left and right of the hidden ones.

- To show hidden rows, select the rows immediately above and below the hidden ones.

- **Format - Row** or **Column** or right-click one of the selected row or column headings.

- Click the **Unhide** option.

    *This method does not allow you to unhide column **A** and/or row **1**. To do this, use the technique performed with the mouse (explained above).*

- **Freezing/unfreezing rows and/or columns**

    This action fixes certain rows or columns on the screen in order to see two sets of data that are far apart on a worksheet.

    - To freeze the column that contains the row titles, make sure that this column is the first one which appears on the left of the screen (if you need to freeze more than one column, make sure that the first of them is displayed at the very left of the screen). To freeze the row which contains column titles, make sure that it is displayed right at the top of the screen (if there are several rows to freeze, the first of them should appear at the top).

    - When the screen is displayed satisfactorily, click a cell in the column after the column(s) to freeze and/or click a cell in the row underneath the row(s) to freeze.

    - **Window - Freeze Panes**

MOUS
Excel 2000 Core

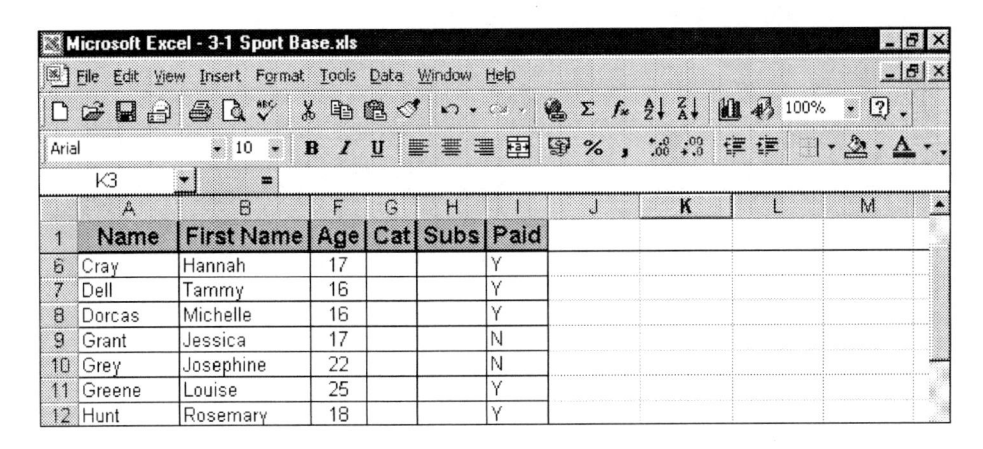

	A	B	F	G	H	I	J	K	L	M
1	Name	First Name	Age	Cat	Subs	Paid				
6	Cray	Hannah	17			Y				
7	Dell	Tammy	16			Y				
8	Dorcas	Michelle	16			Y				
9	Grant	Jessica	17			N				
10	Grey	Josephine	22			N				
11	Greene	Louise	25			Y				
12	Hunt	Rosemary	18			Y				

Here, columns A and B have been frozen, as has row 1. You can see that when the sheet is scrolled, column F appears next to column B and row 6 is below row 1.

📄 *To release titles that have been frozen, use **Window - Unfreeze Panes**.*

7 • Changing column width/row height

* Select each column that should have the same width (or each row that should be the same height). If only one row or column is involved, do not select it, merely click any cell inside it.

* Point to the vertical line on the right of one of the selected column headings (or the horizontal line below one of the selected row numbers):

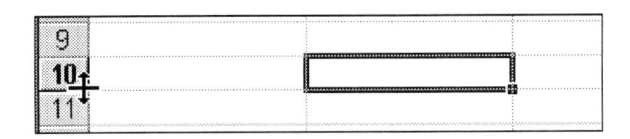

You can see that the pointer has changed shape.

ROWS, COLUMNS AND CELLS
Lesson 3.1: Rows/Columns

- Drag the pointer.

    The new width (or height) is represented by a dotted line, and the value reached as you drag appears in a ScreenTip.

- Release the mouse when you reach the required width (or height).

    The width of a column is calculated as a number of characters (and in pixels) and the height of a row is calculated in points (and in pixels).

    You will save memory by using this method to space out your tables, rather than inserting new rows or columns.

8 • Adjusting columns/rows to fit contents

When you activate this feature, the column width is then calculated according to the longest cell entry in the column and the row height according to the highest cell entry in the row.

- To adjust column width, double-click the vertical line to the right of the letter of the column in question.
  To adjust row height, double-click the horizontal line under the number of the row in question.

MOUS
Excel 2000 Core

Below you can see **Practice Exercise** 3.1. This exercise is made up of 8 steps. If you do not know how to complete one of the steps, go back to the lesson to refer to the corresponding title. When you have finished, check your work by reading the **Solution** on the next page.

Steps that are likely to be tested on the exam are marked with a 🏢 symbol. It is however recommended that you follow the whole exercise in order to gain a complete understanding of the lesson.

☞ Practice Exercise 3.1

In order to complete exercise 3.1, you should open the *3-1 Sport Base.xls* workbook in the ***MOUS Excel 2000*** folder.

1. Select columns **A, B, E** and **F**.

2. Insert three rows after row **6** and one column after column **C**.

3. Delete rows **7, 8** and **9** as well as column **D**.

4. Hide columns **C** and **D**.

5. Unhide columns **C** and **D**.

6. Freeze the titles in columns **A** and **B** as well as the titles in row **1**.

7. Increase the width of column **C** to **23** and height of row **1** to **21**.

8. Adjust columns **D** and **E** to fit their contents.

ROWS, COLUMNS AND CELLS
Exercise 3.1: Rows/Columns

If you want to put what you have learnt into practice on a real document, you can work on summary exercise 3 for the ROWS, COLUMNS AND CELLS section, that you can find at the end of this book.

MOUS
Excel 2000 Core

It is often possible to perform a task in several different ways, but here only the quickest solution is presented. Go back to the lesson to see the other techniques that can be used.

Solution to Exercise 3.1

1. To select columns A, B, E, et F, drag the pointer over the column headings **A** and **B**, hold down the Ctrl key then drag the pointer again from column heading **E** to **F**.

2. To insert three rows after row **6**, select row **6** then point to the fill handle. While holding down the Shift key, drag the fill handle down over three rows.

   To insert a column after column **C**, select column **C** then point to the fill handle.
   While holding down the Shift key, drag the fill handle to the right over one column.

3. To delete rows **7**, **8** and **9**, select rows **7**, **8** and **9** then press Ctrl -.
   To delete column **D**, select column **D** then press Ctrl -.

4. To hide columns **C** and **D**, select columns **C** and **D** then use the **Format - Column - Hide** command.

5. To unhide columns **C** and **D**, select columns **B** and **E** then use the **Format - Column - Unhide** command.

6. To freeze the titles in columns **A** and **B** and those in row **1**, click in cell **C2** then use the **Window - Freeze Panes** command.

ROWS, COLUMNS AND CELLS
Exercise 3.1: Rows/Columns

7. To increase the width of column **C** to **23**, point to the vertical line to the right of the column heading **C**.
   Drag to the right then release the mouse button when the value in the ScreenTip reads **23**.

   To increase the height of row **1** to **21**, point to the horizontal line underneath the number of row **1**.
   Drag downwards then release the mouse button when the value in the ScreenTip reads **21**.

8. To adjust the width of columns **D** and **E** to fit their contents, select columns **D** and **E** then double-click the vertical line on the right of the column **E** heading.

ROWS, COLUMNS AND CELLS
Lesson 3.2: Cells

1. Selecting adjacent cells 66
2. Selecting non-adjacent cells 66
3. Selecting all the cells in a sheet 67
4. Going to a specific cell 67
5. Finding a cell by its contents 68
6. Inserting empty cells 68
7. Moving cells then inserting them 69
8. Deleting cells 69

Practice Exercise 3.2 70

ROWS, COLUMNS AND CELLS
Lesson 3.2: Cells

1 ▪ Selecting adjacent cells

- Use one of the following three techniques:

    Dragging — Click the first cell you want to select then, holding down the mouse button, drag the mouse over the other cells. When you are satisfied with the selection, you can release the mouse button.

    Be careful not to drag the fill handle (the black square in the bottom right corner of the active cell)!

    [Shift]**-clicking** — Click the first cell to be selected and then point to the last cell concerned. Hold down [Shift] and click; release the mouse button then the key.

    Using the keyboard — Hold down the [Shift] key and use the appropriate arrow keys to select the required cells.

Name	First Name	Address	PC/City	Sex	Age
Alderman	Christine	56 Harvey St	4100 Tewesbury	F	13
Andrews	Melissa	27 Ridley St	5600 St Lucia	F	15
Barnett	Frances	38 Harrison Cres	4500 Greerton	F	15
Charles	Yolanda	29 Bartlett Cres	6000 Lorton	F	14
Cray	Hannah	77 Kennedy Drive	5800 Rafter	F	17
Dell	Tammy	13 Read Road	4300 Dryden	F	16
Dorcas	Michelle	10 Kings Ct	5400 Fern Grove	F	16

The selected **cell range** appears in a darker colour except the first cell, which is the active cell and appears like a normal cell.

> By default, the status bar shows the sum of the selected cells.

2 ▪ Selecting non-adjacent cells

- Select the first cell or group of cells.
- Point to the first cell in the next group.

MOUS
Excel 2000 Core

Remember, point but do not click yet!

- Hold down the [Ctrl] key and if necessary, drag to select several cells.
- Release the [Ctrl] key first then the mouse button.

> *In a formula or in a dialog box, a selection of non-adjacent cells is represented by a comma. For example: A5:A10,L5:L10 represents the cell range A5 to A10 and L5 to L10.*

3 ▪ Selecting all the cells in a sheet

- Click the button located at the intersection of the column containing the row numbers and the row containing the column letters or press [Ctrl][Shift][Space] or [Ctrl] A.

4 ▪ Going to a specific cell

- Click in the **Name Box** on the left of the formula bar where the address of the active cell is displayed.

	A	B	C
1	Name	First Name	Address
2	Alderman	Christine	56 Harvey St
3	Andrews	Melissa	27 Ridley St
4	Barnett	Frances	38 Harrison Cres

The reference of the active cell is selected.

- Enter the reference of the cell where you want to go.
- Confirm by pressing ↵.

> *To go to a specific cell, you can also use the **Edit - Go To** command ([Ctrl] G); in the **Reference** text box, enter the reference of the cell where you want to go then click **OK**.*

ROWS, COLUMNS AND CELLS
Lesson 3.2: Cells

5 ▪ Finding a cell by its contents

- **Edit - Go To** or [F5] or [Ctrl] G
- Click the **Special** button.
- Choose the type of cell you want to select.

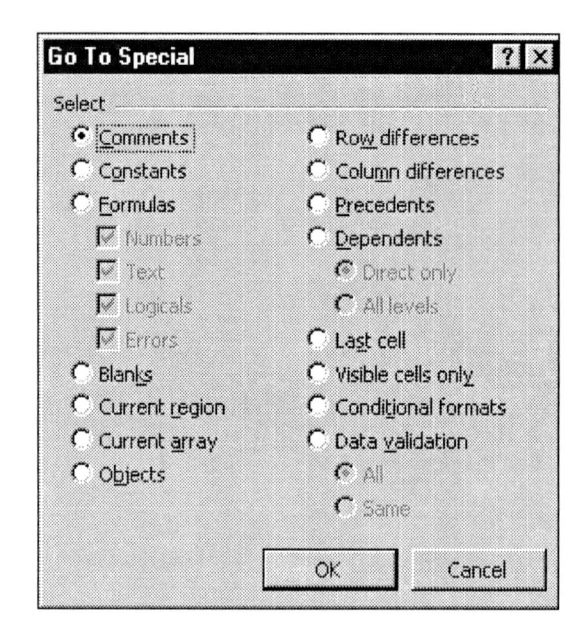

[Go To Special dialog box with options: Comments, Constants, Formulas (Numbers, Text, Logicals, Errors), Blanks, Current region, Current array, Objects, Row differences, Column differences, Precedents, Dependents (Direct only, All levels), Last cell, Visible cells only, Conditional formats, Data validation (All, Same), OK, Cancel]

- Click **OK**.

6 ▪ Inserting empty cells

- Select the cell <u>in front of</u> the place you wish to insert the new cells.
- Hold down [Shift] and drag the fill handle over as many cells as you want to insert new ones.

- Select as many cells as you want to insert of new ones.
- **Insert - Cells** or [Ctrl] +
- Activate the first or second option to indicate how the existing cells should move to make way for the new ones.
- Click **OK**.

7 ▪ Moving cells then inserting them

The cells are moved and inserted between other existing cells.

- Select the cells you want to move.
- Point to one of the edges of the selected range.
- Hold down the [Shift] key and drag the selected cells.
- Release the mouse when you reach the point where the cells will be inserted, symbolised by a thick hatched line.

8 ▪ Deleting cells

- Select the cells you want to delete.
- Hold down the [Shift] key and drag the fill handle up over the selection.

    *Deleting in this way moves the remaining cells upwards. If you want the remaining cells to moved to the left, use the **Edit - Delete** command or use the [Ctrl][-] keys.*

ROWS, COLUMNS AND CELLS
Exercise 3.2: Cells

Below you can see **Practice Exercise** 3.2. This exercise is made up of 8 steps. If you do not know how to complete one of the steps, go back to the lesson to refer to the corresponding title. When you have finished, check your work by reading the **Solution** on the next page.

Steps that are likely to be tested on the exam are marked with a 🖽 symbol. It is however recommended that you follow the whole exercise in order to gain a complete understanding of the lesson.

☞ Practice Exercise 3.2

In order to complete exercise 3.2, you should open the *3-2 Sport Base.xls* workbook in the **MOUS Excel 2000** folder.

1. Select cells **A2** to **B47**.

2. Select cells **E2** to **F47** and **I2** to **I47**.

3. Select all the cells on the worksheet.

🖽 4. Go to cell **C45**.

5. Go to the blank cells in the list of data.

🖽 6. Insert three empty cells underneath cell **D4**.

🖽 7. Move cell **C7** and insert it between cells **C8** and **C9**.

🖽 8. Delete cells **D5** to **D7**.

If you want to put what you have learnt into practice on a real document, you can work on summary exercise 3 for ROWS, COLUMNS AND CELLS section, that you can find at the end of this book.

It is often possible to perform a task in several different ways, but here only the quickest solution is presented. Go back to the lesson to see the other techniques that can be used.

Solution to Exercise 3.2

1. To select cells A2 to B47, click in cell **A2** then hold down the mouse button and drag the mouse to cell **B47**.

2. To select cells E2 to F47 and I2 to I47, start by selecting the range of cells **E2** to **F47**.
   Point to cell **I2** then hold down the [Ctrl] key and select the cell range **I2** to **I47**.

3. To select all the cells on the worksheet, press [Ctrl] **A**.

4. To go to cell **C45**, click the **Name Box** on the left of the formula bar where the reference of the active cell is displayed.
   Type **C45** then [↵] on the keyboard.

5. To select the empty cells in the data list, use the **Edit - Go To** command and click the **Special** button.
   Activate the **Blanks** option then click **OK**.

6. To insert three empty cells below cell D4, click cell **D4** to select it.
   Hold down the [Shift] key and drag the fill handle downward over three cells.

ROWS, COLUMNS AND CELLS
Exercise 3.2: Cells

7. To move cell C7 and insert it between cells C8 and C9, click cell **C7** to select it.
   Point to one of the edges of cell **C7** then hold down the [Shift] key. Drag the selected cell between cells **C8** and **C9**: the place where the cells will be inserted is symbolised by a thick hatched line.
   Release the mouse button then the [Shift] key.

8. To delete cells D5 to D7, select them.
   Point to the fill handle then hold down the [Shift] key and drag the fill handle upwards over cells **D7** to **D5**.
   Release the mouse button then the [Shift] key.

MANAGING DATA
Lesson 4.1: Entering data

1 - Entering constants (text, values, dates) 74

2 - Entering several lines of text in one cell 76

3 - Creating a data series 76

4 - Creating a custom data series 77

5 - Establishing a hyperlink with another document 78

Practice Exercise 4.1 80

MANAGING DATA
Lesson 4.1: Entering data

1 ▪ Entering constants (text, values, dates)

- Activate the cell where you want to display the data.

    *You should always check the active cell reference in the **Name Box** on the left of the formula bar.*

- Enter the data.

	A	B	C	D	E	F	G
B7		× ✓ = 4185					
1							
2							
3							
4	SALESPEOPLE						
5		5680	5290	5284			
6		4575	4796	4400			
7		4185		4050	5125			
8	TOTAL	10255	14136	14809			
9		5680	5290	5284			

    Once you have entered the first character, two symbols appear in the formula bar:

    ☒ to cancel the entry (corresponds to the Esc key).

    ☑ to confirm the entry (corresponds to the ⏎ key).

    At the same time, the word "Enter" appears on the status bar to indicate that only data entry can be performed.

- Activate next cell where you wish to enter data.

    The act of going to a new cell confirms the previous entry. Once you activate a new cell (with the mouse or using one of the arrow keys), Excel returns to Ready mode and the ☒ and ☑ symbols disappear.

    Once confirmed, Text type data is left aligned in the cells, and Date or Number type data are aligned on the right of the cells. In addition to this, Date type data are formatted (for example, 12/01 becomes 12-Jan or 01-Dec, depending on your computer's regional settings).

MOUS
Excel 2000 Core

- Continue with your other data entry.

  *It is essential to confirm the last item entered before returning to **Ready** mode.*

- When entering data, you should keep the following observations in mind:

  - You can type up to 32000 characters of text in each cell.
  - With numerical data, be careful to type in 0 (zero) and not O (the letter o).
  - Negative values can be indicated by either preceding them with a minus sign (-) or by placing them within brackets.
  - If you enter £10000 or $10000, Excel immediately applies a £10,000 or $10,000 format.
  - To enter a percentage, type a % sign just after the number.
  - To enter decimals, use a decimal point as separator (this should be the decimal separator specified in your Windows Regional Settings).

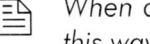

  When dates are entered, Excel interprets years entered as two numbers in this way:
  - from 00 to 29 as the years 2000 to 2029,
  - from 30 to 99 as the years 1930 to 1999.

  *If you use Windows 98, Windows 2000 or a later version, these parameters can be modified in the Windows regional settings, in the **Start** menu, under **Settings - Control Panel - Regional Settings - Date** tab. If you use Windows 95 or earlier, you can download a special tool which will update the year settings, by connecting to the Microsoft site (http://www.microsoft.com/office/ork/2000).*

  To insert your computer's control date, press `Ctrl` `;`. *This date is not automatically updated when the workbook is opened.*

MANAGING DATA
Lesson 4.1: Entering data

2 ▪ Entering several lines of text in one cell

- Activate the cell that you want to fill in.
- Enter the cell contents, pressing [Alt][↵] whenever you want to insert a line break.

	A			
1	TOTAL SALES PER SALESPERSON			
2				
3				
4	SALESPEOPLE			
5		5680	5290	5284
6		4575	4796	4400
7		4185	4050	5125
8	TOTAL	14440	14136	14809
9	Best result	5680	5290	5284

- Press [↵] to confirm.

> The **Wrap text** option also uses several lines to display the contents of a cell but Excel defines the line breaks automatically to fit the text to the column.

3 ▪ Creating a data series

A data series is a logical progression. Here is an example of a simple data series:

	A	B	C	D
3				
4	SALESPEOPLE	APRIL	MAY	JUNE
5		5680	5290	5284
6		4575	4796	4400

"Simple" data series

- Enter the first value in the series.
- Drag the fill handle from the active cell to the cell where the last value in the series is to be shown.

"Complex" data series

- Instead of entering just the first value in the data series, enter the first two.
- Select these two cells.
- Drag the fill handle as for a simple series.

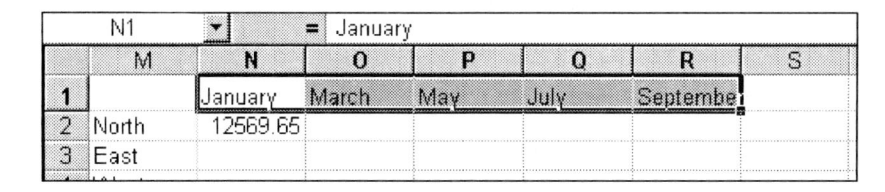

January and March were selected to create this "complex" series.

4 ▪ Creating a custom data series

- **Tools - Options - Custom Lists** tab
- In the **Custom lists** box, click **NEW LIST** even if this choice has already been selected.

  The insertion point appears in the List entries box.

- In the **List entries** box, enter each item of data, separating each by pressing ↵.

MANAGING DATA
Lesson 4.1: Entering data

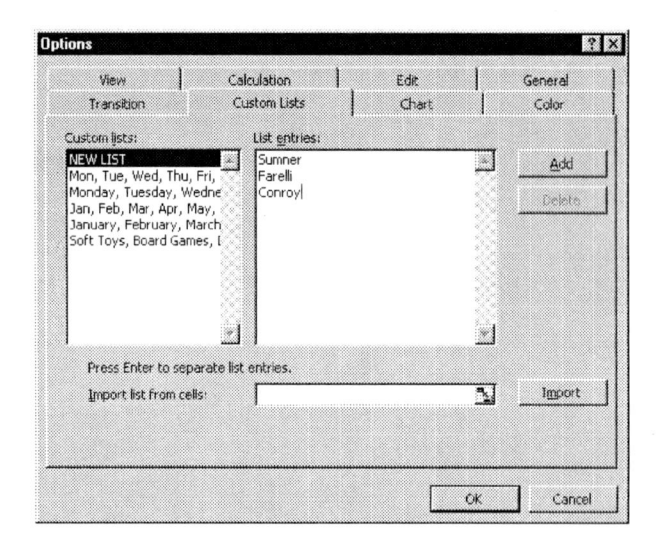

- Click the **Add** button.

  The new list appears among the current custom lists: each entry is separated from the previous one by a comma.

- Press **OK** to confirm.

- To insert a custom data series, click the first required cell and enter one of the list values. Drag the fill handle from the active cell to the cell where the last value is to be shown.

5 ▪ Establishing a hyperlink with another document

- Select the cell where you wish the hyperlink to be placed

- **Insert - Hyperlink** or [icon] or Ctrl K

- If necessary, activate the **Existing File or Web Page** shortcut in the left part of the dialog box.

- In the **Type the file or Web page name** text box, indicate the name of the document with which you want to establish a link. You can also use the **File** button to select the document.

This document can be either a document located on a workstation drive or an Internet address.

- To access a particular place in the document directly, use the **Bookmark** button and select the name of the item you want to go to.

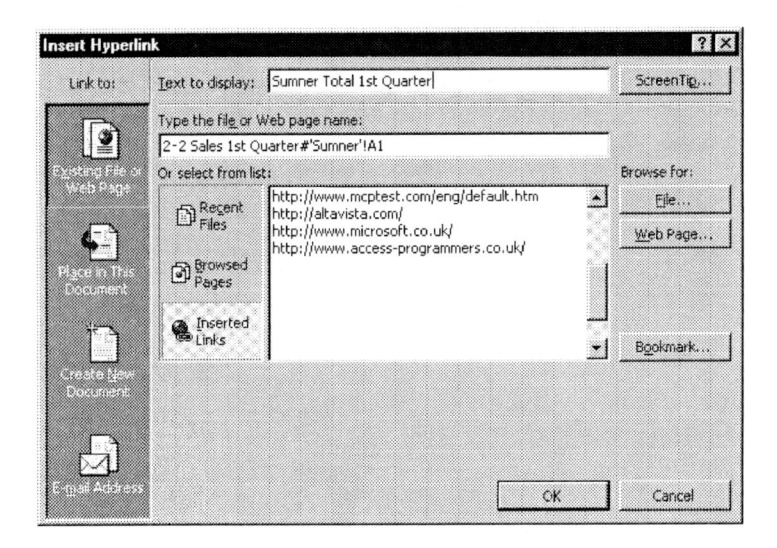

You can use the name of a worksheet, a range of named cells...

- Click **OK** to create the link.

- To open the document associated with the link, click the link when the pointer takes the shape of a hand.

    The document appears on the screen along with the Web toolbar (if the Web toolbar does not appear, you can display it using **View - Toolbars - Web**).

- Click the ⬅ tool to return to the original document.

    Both documents stay open.

    When you return to the workbook after having consulted the linked document, the hyperlink appears in purple.

    To delete a hyperlink, select the cell containing it and press the Del key.

MANAGING DATA
Exercise 4.1: Entering Data

Below you can see **Practice Exercise** 4.1. This exercise is made up of 5 steps. If you do not know how to complete one of the steps, go back to the lesson to refer to the corresponding title. When you have finished, check your work by reading the **Solution** on the next page.

Steps that are likely to be tested on the exam are marked with a 🏢 symbol. It is however recommended that you follow the whole exercise in order to gain a complete understanding of the lesson.

☞ Practice Exercise 4.1

In order to complete exercise 4.1, you should open the **4-1 Sales 2nd Quarter.xls** workbook in the **MOUS Excel 2000** folder then activate the **Sheet1** worksheet.

🏢 1. Enter this text:
   - **TOTAL SALES PER SALESPERSON** in cell **A1**.
   - **4185** in cell **B7**.
   - **8/7/00** in cell **B12**.

2. Enter **Best Result** over two lines in cell **A9**.

🏢 3. Create the data series **APRIL, MAY** and **JUNE** in cells **B4** to **D4**.

🏢 4. Create a custom data series containing the names **SUMNER, FARELLI** and **CONROY**. Insert this list into cells **A5** to **A7**.

🏢 5. In cell **A15**, insert a hyperlink that accesses the **2-2 Sales 1st Quarter.xls** workbook in the **MOUS Excel 2000** folder. Go into that document then return to the **4-1 Sales 2nd Quarter.xls** workbook.

If you want to put what you have learnt into practice on a real document, you can work on summary exercise 4 for the MANAGING DATA section, that you can find at the end of this book.

MOUS
Excel 2000 Core

It is often possible to perform a task in several different ways, but here only the quickest solution is presented. Go back to the lesson to see the other techniques that can be used.

Solution to Exercise 4.1

1. To enter the text TOTAL SALES PER SALESPERSON into cell A1, click in cell **A1**, type **TOTAL SALES PER SALESPERSON** then confirm with the ⏎ key.

   To enter the value 4185 into cell B7, click cell **B7**, type **41850** then confirm by pressing ⏎.

   To enter the date 8/7/00 into cell B12, click cell **B12**, type **8/7/00** then confirm by pressing ⏎.

2. To enter Best Result over two lines in cell A9, click cell **A9** to select it.
   Type **Best** then press [Alt] ⏎ to insert a line break.
   Type **Result** then press ⏎ to confirm.

3. To create the data series APRIL, MAY and JUNE in cells B4 to D4, click cell **B4** then type **APRIL**.
   Point to the fill handle on cell **B4** then drag it over cells **C4** and **D4**.

4. To create a custom data series containing the names SUMNER, FARELLI and CONROY, use the **Tools - Options** command then click the **Custom Lists** tab.
   Click the **NEW LIST** option in the **Custom lists** list box.
   In the **List entries** box, enter **SUMNER, FARELLI** and **CONROY** separating each name with ⏎.
   Click the **Add** button then click **OK**.
   To insert the list in cells A5 to A7, click cell **A5**, type **SUMNER** then confirm with ⏎.
   Select cell **A5**, point to the fill handle then drag it over cells **A6** and **A7**.

81

MANAGING DATA
Exercise 4.1: Entering Data

5. To create a hyperlink to **2-2 Sales 1st Quarter** in cell **A15**, go to cell **A15** and use the **Insert - Hyperlink** command then if necessary, activate the **Existing File or Web Page** shortcut.
Click the **File** button then double-click the **2-2 Sales 1st Quarter** workbook in the **MOUS Excel 2000** folder. Click **OK** to create the link.

To go to the **2-2 Sales 1st Quarter.xls** workbook, double-click the link when the pointer takes the shape of a hand.

To return to the **4-1 Sales 2nd Quarter.xls** workbook, click the ⇐ tool on the **Web** toolbar.

MANAGING DATA
Lesson 4.2: Modifying data

1. Modifying cell contents 84

2. Clearing cell contents 84

3. Clearing a cell's format 85

4. Looking for a cell with a particular content 85

5. Replacing cell contents 87

6. Checking the spelling of a text 88

Practice Exercise 4.2 90

MANAGING DATA
Lesson 4.2: Modifying data

1 • Modifying cell contents

▫ Double-click the cell you wish to modify:

	A	B	C	D
1	SALES - SUMNER			
2				

A1 ▼ X ✓ = SALES - SUMNER

An insertion point (the flashing vertical bar) appears in the cell and Excel displays **Edit** *on the status bar.*

▫ Make your changes.

The new characters entered are added to the existing characters, providing Insert mode is active. If Overtype mode is active, the new characters replace the existing ones.

▫ To go from Insert to Overtype mode, and vice versa, press the [Inser] key.

▫ Confirm your changes by pressing the ↵ key.

📄 *You can also click the cell then make your modifications directly in the formula bar.*

2 • Clearing cell contents

▫ Select the cells you want to clear.

▫ Drag the selection's fill handle over all the cells you want to clear.

While you drag, the cells appear in grey then the cell contents disappear.

📄 *Like pressing the [Del] key, this technique removes the contents of the cell but not its format.*

MOUS
Excel 2000 Core

3 ▪ Clearing a cell's format

The cell contents are not deleted, but the formatting is (character formats, borders...).

▪ Select the cells concerned.

▪ Open the **Edit** menu and point to the **Clear** option.

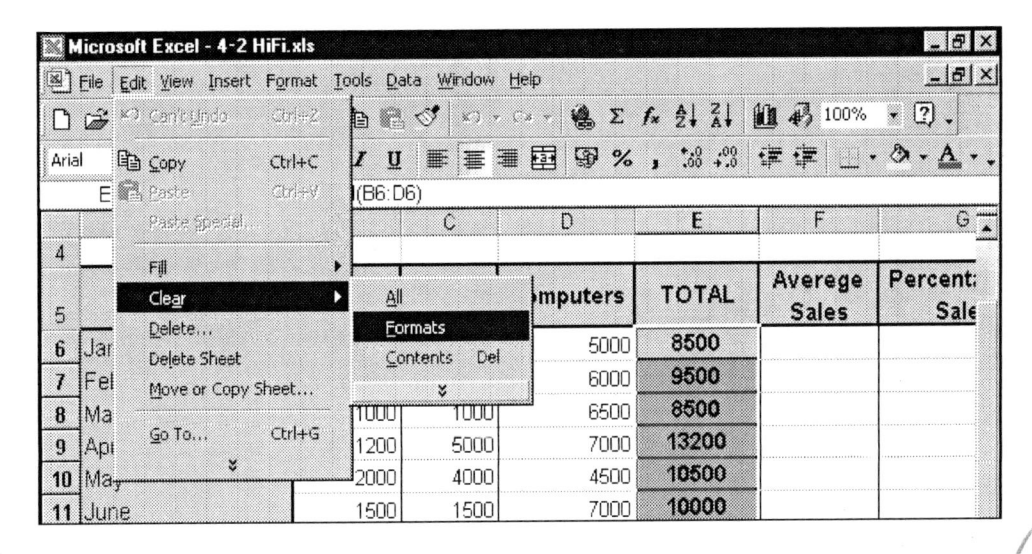

▪ Click the **Formats** option.

4 ▪ Looking for a cell with a particular content

▪ If the search is to be carried out over the whole sheet, activate cell A1; if you want to search in one particular section only, select that section.

▪ **Edit - Find** or Ctrl F

▪ Enter what you are looking for in the **Find what** text box.

▪ In the **Search** list box, select the direction in which the search should be made.

MANAGING DATA
Lesson 4.2: Modifying data

- In the **Look in** list box, select the worksheet element containing the information for which you are looking.
- Activate the **Match case** option if you want the search to distinguish between upper and lower case characters.
- Activate the **Find entire cells only** if you want Excel to search for cells whose contents match precisely the characters entered in the **Find what** box.
- Start searching by clicking the **Find Next** button.

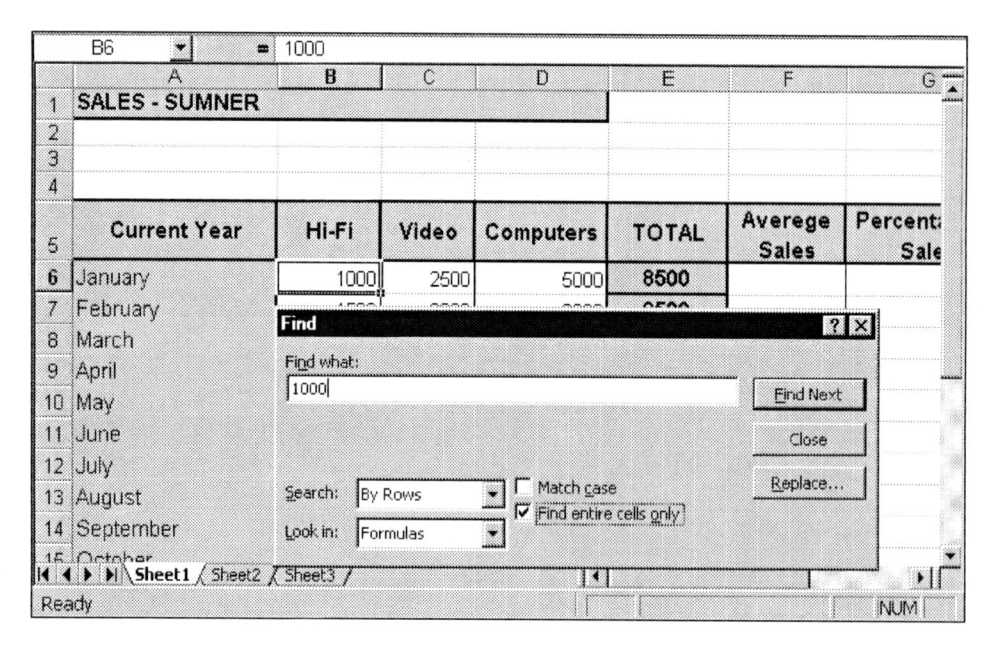

- If the first cell found contains the item you are looking for, click the **Close** button to close the dialog box; if not, click **Find Next** again to continue searching.

When the **Find** dialog box is closed, you can continue the last search started by pressing Shift F4.

5 ▪ Replacing cell contents

This action allows you to automatically replace the contents of certain cells with other texts.

- Select the cells concerned.
- **Edit - Replace** or **Ctrl H**
- Enter the text you want to replace in the **Find what** box.

  *This box can contain letters, numbers, punctuation marks or wildcards (? or * replace one or more characters in your search criterion). No distinction is made between upper and lower case characters unless you activate the **Match case** option.*

- Press **Tab** and enter the replacement text in the **Replace with** text box.

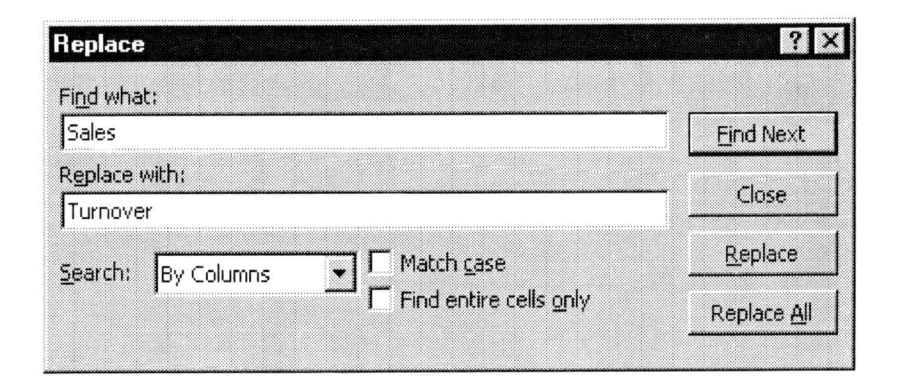

- Make your replacements one by one using the **Find Next** and **Replace** buttons or in one single action with the **Replace All** button.

MANAGING DATA
Lesson 4.2: Modifying data

6 ▪ Checking the spelling of a text

- To check the spelling over a whole worksheet, activate any cell. To check a range of cells containing text, select those cells.

- **Tools - Spelling** or ![ABC✓] or F7

    Excel examines the text and stops when it reaches an unknown word. A word is unknown if it is:

    - not included in the dictionary used by Excel,

    - entered with an unusual combination of upper and lower case letters (for example, SAles),

    - repeated (for example, that that one is...).

    A list of suggested corrections for the detected mistake is offered if the **Always suggest** option is active. This check is made from the main dictionary (from Excel) and as many custom dictionaries as you like (by default, the only existing one is CUSTOM.DIC).

- If the word is correctly spelt, click:

    Ignore   to leave the word unchanged and continue checking.

    Ignore All   to ignore the word here and every time it occurs subsequently.

    Add   to add the word to the active dictionary.

- If the word is incorrect, you can correct it by selecting one of the suggestions or by entering the correct text in the **Replace with** text box and clicking:

    Change   to replace the incorrect word with the entered one.

    Change All   to replace the word here, and every time it occurs, with the entered text.

- In the case of a repeated word, click the **Delete** button to remove it.

- When Excel has finished checking, the following dialog box appears:

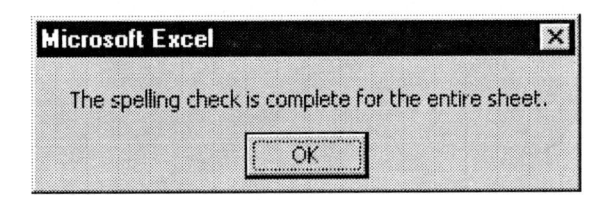

  > **Microsoft Excel**
  > The spelling check is complete for the entire sheet.
  > [OK]

- Click **OK**.

  > *To create a custom dictionary, select the active dictionary in the **Spelling** dialog box, type the name of the new dictionary and confirm.*

MANAGING DATA
Exercise 4.2: Modifying data

Below, you can see **Practice Exercise** 4.2. This exercise is made up of 6 steps. If you do not know how to complete one of the steps, go back to the lesson to refer to the corresponding title. When you have finished, check your work by reading the **Solution** on the next page.

All the steps in this exercice are likely to be tested in the exam.

☞ Practice Exercise 4.2

In order to complete exercise 4.2, you should open the **4-2 Hi-Fi.xls** worksheet in the **MOUS Excel 2000** folder then activate **Sheet1** if necessary.

1. Change the text in cell **A1** to **SALES FIGURES FOR SUMNER**. ✓

2. Clear the contents of cells **A20** to **D21**. ✓

3. Clear the format of cells **E6** to **E17**. ✓

4. Look for the cells containing a value of **1000**. ✓

5. In cells **F5** and **G5** replace the word **Sales** by the word **Turnover**. ✓

6. Check the spelling of all the texts on **Sheet1** and make any necessary changes.

If you want to put what you have learnt into practice on a real document, you can work on summary exercise 4 for the MANAGING DATA section, that you can find at the end of this book.

MOUS
Excel 2000 Core

It is often possible to perform a task in several different ways, but here only the quickest solution is presented. Go back to the lesson to see the other techniques that can be used.

Solution to Exercise 4.2

1. To change the text in A1 to **SALES FIGURES FOR SUMNER**, double-click cell **A1**.
   Place the insertion point before the hyphen and press the [Del] key.
   Enter **FIGURES FOR** then confirm by pressing ↵.

2. To clear the contents of cells A20 to D21, select cells **A20** to **D21** then press [Del].

3. To clear the format of cells E6 to E17, select cells **E6** to **E17**, open the **Edit** menu then point to the **Clear** option.
   Click the **Formats** option.

4. To look for the cells containing the value 1000, click in cell **A1** then use the **Edit - Find** command.
   Enter **1000** in the **Find what** text box then activate the **Find entire cells only** option.
   Click the **Find Next** button to start the search and see the first cell found.
   Click the **Find Next** button several times to see the other cells containing the value **1000**.
   When the search is finished, click the **Close** button.

MANAGING DATA
Exercise 4.2: Modifying data

5. To replace the text **Sales** in cells F5 and G5 with **Turnover**, click cell **A1** then use the **Edit - Replace** command.
   Type **Sales** in the **Find what** text box then **Turnover** in the **Replace with** text box.
   If necessary, deactivate the **Find entire cells only** option and the **Match case** option.
   Click the **Find Next** button twice, then click the **Change** button twice then the **Close** button.

6. To check the spelling of the text in **Sheet1** click cell **A1** of **Sheet1** then use the **Tools - Spelling** command.
   Click the **Ignore** button then **Replace** twice.
   Click the **OK** button when the spelling check is finished.

MANAGING DATA
Lesson 4.3: Copying and moving

- 1 ▪ Copying cell contents to adjacent cells 94
- 2 ▪ Copying/moving cells 94
- 3 ▪ Making multiple moves/copies with the Office Clipboard 96
- 4 ▪ Copying calculation results or formats 97
- 5 ▪ Copying and transposing data 98
- 6 ▪ Copying cells and establishing a link 98
- 7 ▪ Making simple calculations during copying 99

Practice Exercise 4.3 101

MANAGING DATA
Lesson 4.3: Copying and moving

1 • Copying cell contents to adjacent cells

- Click the cell whose contents are to be copied.
- Point to the cell's fill handle:

AVERAGE	PROGRESSION
5236	-2%
	13%
	-13%

The fill handle is the small black square in the active cell's bottom right corner. Notice how, when you point to it, the pointer changes shape.

- Hold down the mouse button and drag towards the destination cell for the copy.

  The cells over which you drag appear with a hatched border.
- When the last destination cell is reached, release the mouse button.

2 • Copying/moving cells

These copying techniques are used to move or copy into non-adjacent cells.

First method

This technique is usually used when the copied cells and destination cells can both be viewed on the same screen.

- Select the cells you wish to move or copy.

- Point to one of the edges of the selected group.

	A	B	C	D
1		SALES RESULTS PER VENDOR		
2				
3				
4		Rate of commission	10%	
5				

The pointer takes the shape of a white arrow. Be careful not to point to the fill handle!

- If you are making a copy, hold down the [Ctrl] key and drag the cells towards their new destination.

  If you wish to just move the cells, drag them towards the first destination cell.

  When you make a copy, a small plus sign (+) appears to the right of the pointer.

- Release the mouse button, then, if you have been using it, the [Ctrl] key.

Second method

- Select the cells you want to move or copy.
- If you wish to copy the cells, use **Edit - Copy** or [icon] or [Ctrl] C
- If you wish to move the cells, use **Edit - Cut** or [icon] or [Ctrl] X

  *The selected cells appear in a flashing border. They have been copied or moved into the Windows clipboard. The **Clipboard** toolbar may also appear on the screen.*

- Activate the first destination cell for the moved/copied data.

  Even if you are moving/copying several cells, only one destination cell needs to be activated.

MANAGING DATA
Lesson 4.3: Copying and moving

- **Edit - Paste** or 🗐 or `Ctrl` **V**

  > *The selected cells are still in the clipboard and you can paste them into other positions if you wish.*
  > *To copy a group of cells into another worksheet, you can use the first method: hold down the `Ctrl` and `Alt` keys then drag the selection first to the destination worksheet tab then onto the first destination cell.*

3 ▪ Making multiple moves/copies with the Office Clipboard

- Display, if necessary, the **Clipboard** toolbar by using the command **View - Toolbars - Clipboard**.

  This toolbar may be displayed automatically when you make two copies consecutively.

- Select the cells concerned then transfer them to the clipboard with the **Cut** or **Copy** commands. Carry out this action as many times as is necessary.

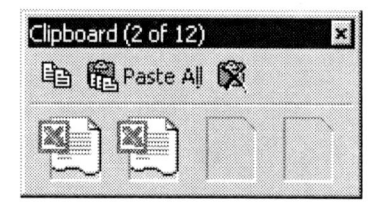

  *The selected items appear as icons on the **Clipboard** toolbar (up to 12 items can be copied onto the clipboard).*

- Activate the first destination cell.
- To paste one of the selected items from the **Clipboard** toolbar, click its icon.

  When you point to the icon, without clicking, a ScreenTip appears showing the first fifty characters of the copied item (or the item number if it is an object or picture).

- Insert each item from the **Clipboard** toolbar in this way, as many times as you like.

   When you paste an item from the Clipboard toolbar onto another sheet, the values and formats are retrieved but not the formulas contained in the original cells.

- Close the **Clipboard** toolbar by clicking the ☒ button or by deactivating the **Clipboard** option in the **View - Toolbars** menu.

   The **Paste All** *button on the **Clipboard** toolbar pastes in all the items on the toolbar. They are copied in a column, one underneath the other. This button is not available if one of the elements is an image or object.*

   *To empty the **Clipboard**, click the ☒ tool on the **Clipboard** toolbar. The clipboard is also emptied when you close all Microsoft Office applications (Word, Excel, PowerPoint, Access ...).*

4 ▪ Copying calculation results or formats

- Select the cells containing the results or formats you want to copy.
- Proceed as for an ordinary copy (**Edit - Copy**).
- Activate the first destination cell for the copy.
- **Edit - Paste Special**
- If you only want to copy calculation results, choose the **Values** option. If you only want to copy formats, choose the **Formats** option.
- Click **OK**.
- Press `Esc` on the keyboard to deactivate the copying process.

   The ⌘ tool can also be used to copy the presentation of one cell onto other cells (cf. Lesson 6.1 – 9. Copying formats).

MANAGING DATA
Lesson 4.3: Copying and moving

5 ▪ Copying and transposing data

This technique is used to transpose the columns and rows on a table when you copy it (the rows become columns and the columns become rows).

- Select the data you want to copy, start copying (**Edit - Copy**), then activate the first destination cell for the copy.
- **Edit - Paste Special**
- Under **Paste** specify what you want to copy.
- Activate the **Transpose** option.
- Click **OK**.

When you do this the rows become columns and vice versa.

- Press `Esc` on the keyboard to deactivate the copying process.

6 ▪ Copying cells and establishing a link

- Select the data you wish to copy.
- Start copying (**Edit - Copy**).
- Activate the first destination cell for the copy.
- **Edit - Paste Special**
- Click the **Paste Link** button.

The destination cells now contain a formula that displays the contents of each source cell. If you modify a source value, the contents of the corresponding target cell are automatically modified.

MOUS
Excel 2000 Core

> *Creating a link when you paste does not allow you to retrieve formatting immediately.*
> *If you paste an empty cell with a link, Excel displays a zero.*
> *You can obtain the same result by inserting in the destination cell a format of this type: =cell.*

7 ▪ Making simple calculations during copying

This action lets you copy data and at the same time perform an operation (addition, subtraction...) combining the copied data and the data contained in the destination cells.

- Select the data you wish to copy and start copying (**Edit - Copy**).
- Activate the first destination cell (the destination cells must contain data).
- **Edit - Paste Special**

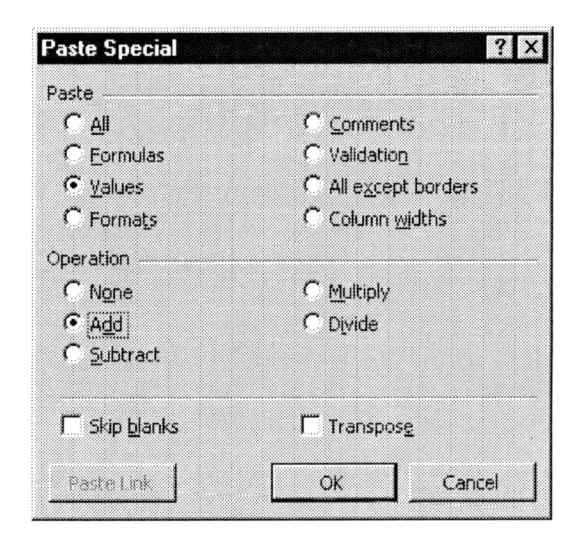

99

MANAGING DATA
Lesson 4.3: Copying and moving

- Under **Paste**, indicate whether you want to copy **Formulas** or **Values**.
- Click the option corresponding to the **Operation** you want to perform.
- If any empty cells present in the selection should be left out, activate the **Skip blanks** option.
- Click **OK**.
- Press [Esc] on the keyboard to deactivate the copying process.

MOUS
Excel 2000 Core

Below you can see **Practice Exercise** 4.3. This exercise is made up of 7 steps. If you do not know how to complete one of the steps, go back to the lesson to refer to the corresponding title. When you have finished, check your work by reading the **Solution** on the next page.

All the steps in this exercise are likely to be tested in the exam.

☞ Practice Exercise 4.3

*In order to complete exercise 4.3, you should open the **4-3 Sales Progression.xls** workbook located in the **MOUS Excel 2000** folder.*

1. In the **Progression** worksheet, copy the contents of cell **D6** into the adjacent cells **D7** and **D8**.

2. In the **Results** worksheet, move cells **B4** and **C4** towards cells **A4** and **B4**.

3. Copy cells **A6** to **A8** and **C6** to **C8** on the **Progression** sheet then paste them into cells **A8** to **A10** and **B8** to **B10** on the **Results** sheet, using the Office 2000 clipboard.

4. On the **Results** worksheet, copy the format of cell **D7** onto cells **B7** and **C7**.

5. Copy cells **A7** to **D11** on the **Results** sheet them paste them, transposing the data, onto the **Transpose** worksheet. The first destination cell for the copy should be cell **A3**.

MANAGING DATA
Exercise 4.3: Copying and moving

6. Copy cells **A8** to **A10** on the **Results** worksheet onto cells **A5** to **A7** on the **Vendor Totals** sheet, establishing a link with the copy.

7. On the **Vendor Totals** sheet, make a copy of cells **B5** to **B7** onto cells **C5** to **C7** adding the values from January to those from February (the values that you can see currently in cells **C5** to **C7** correspond to the January sales turnover).

If you want to put what you have learnt into practice on a real document, you can work on summary exercise 4 for the MANAGING DATA section, that you can find at the end of this book.

MOUS
Excel 2000 Core

It is often possible to perform a task in several different ways, but here only the quickest solution is presented. Go back to the lesson to see the other techniques that can be used.

Solution to Exercise 4.3

1. To copy the contents of cell **D6** into the adjacent cells **D7** and **D8** on the **Progression** sheet, click the **Progression** sheet tab, then click cell **D6**. Point to the fill handle on cell **D6**, then drag the fill handle down to cell **D8**.

2. To move cells **B4** and **C4** to cells **A4** and **B4** on the **Results** sheet, click the **Results** tab then select cells **B4** and **C4**.
   Point to one of the edges of the selected range then drag it to cell **A4**.

3. To copy cells **A6** to **A8** and **C6** to **C8** on the **Progression** sheet then paste them onto cells **A8** to **A10** and **B8** to **B10** on the **Results** sheet, start by displaying the **Clipboard** toolbar with the **View - Toolbars - Clipboard** command.

   Click the **Progression** tab, select cells **A6** to **A8** and click the [icon] tool then select cells **C6** to **C8** and click [icon] again.

   Click the **Results** tab.
   Click cell **A8** then the first icon on the **Clipboard** toolbar to paste the first cell range.
   Click cell **B8** then the second icon on the **Clipboard** toolbar to paste the second cell range.

103

MANAGING DATA
Exercise 4.3: Copying and moving

4. To copy the format of cell **D7** onto cells **B7** and **C7** on the **Results** sheet, click the **Results** tab then cell **D7**.

   Click the [icon] tool then select cells **B7** and **C7**.
   Use the **Edit - Paste Special** command, activate the **Formats** option in the **Paste** frame then click **OK**.
   Press [Esc] to deactivate the copying process.

5. To copy cells **A7** to **D11** on the **Results** worksheet and paste them, transposing the data, onto the **Transpose** sheet, click the **Results** sheet tab then select cells **A7** to **D11**.

   Click the [icon] tool then the **Transpose** tab.

   Click cell **A3** then use the **Edit - Paste Special** command. Activate the **Transpose** option in the bottom part of the dialog box then click **OK**.
   Press [Esc] to deactivate the copying process.

6. To copy cells **A8** to **A10** on the **Results** sheet to cells **A5** to **A7** on the **Vendor Totals** sheet, and establish a link between the cells, start by clicking the **Results** tab.

   Select cells **A8** to **A10**, click the [icon] tool then the **Vendor Totals** tab.

   Click cell **A5**, use the **Edit - Paste Special** command then click the **Paste Link** button.

7. To copy cells **B5** to **B7** onto cells **C5** to **C7**, adding the values from January to those for February, click the **Vendor Totals** tab.

   Select cells **B5** to **B7** then click the [icon] tool.

   Select cells **C5** to **C7** then use the **Edit - Paste Special** command. Activate the **Add** option in the **Operation** frame then click **OK**.
   Press [Esc] to deactivate the copying process.

CALCULATIONS
Lesson 5.1: Formulas

- 1 ▪ Entering calculation formulas 106
- 2 ▪ Modifying formulas 108
- 3 ▪ Using AutoSum 108
- 4 ▪ Including absolute cell references in a formula 109

Practice Exercise 5.1 111

CALCULATIONS
Lesson 5.1: Formulas

1 ▪ Entering calculation formulas

- Activate the cell which will display the result.
- Type =

  The word **Enter** appears on the status bar.

- Activate the first cell involved in the calculation.

  This cell is shown with a flashing border and its reference appears in the formula bar. The status bar now shows you are in **Point** mode.

- Type in the mathematical operation to be carried out:

+	for addition
-	for subtraction
/	for division
*	for multiplication
%	for percentage
^	to raise to a power (exponentiation)

- Repeat for each of the cells involved in the calculation, entering the appropriate operator.

  You can follow the development of the formula on the formula bar:

AVERAGE	▼	X	✓	=	=D5*E5		
	B	C	D	E	F	G
1	RDERS FOR 1ST SEMESTER					
2						
3						
4	COST PRICE	SALE PRICE	PROFIT MARGIN	QUANTITY	PROFIT MADE	SHARE OF PROFIT
5	207.00	258.75	51.75	25	=D5*E5	
6	449.00	538.80	89.80	18		

MOUS
Excel 2000 Core

- When you reach the last cell, press the ↵ key to confirm your formula.

    The calculation result appears in the cell but the cell's true content is the formula, which is displayed in the formula bar when the cell is active.

    📄 *A calculation formula can contain up to 1024 characters.*

    📌 *If you know the cell references, you can type them in rather than using the mouse or arrow keys to activate them.*

🖱 *With the mouse, you can use the formula palette to enter a formula.*

- Activate the cell which will display the result.
- Click the = button on the formula bar.

    *The formula palette is made up of the formula bar and the grey area containing the **OK** and **Cancel** buttons.*

- Click the first cell you want to include in the formula.
- Type in the appropriate mathematical operator.
- Continue entering the formula in the same way:

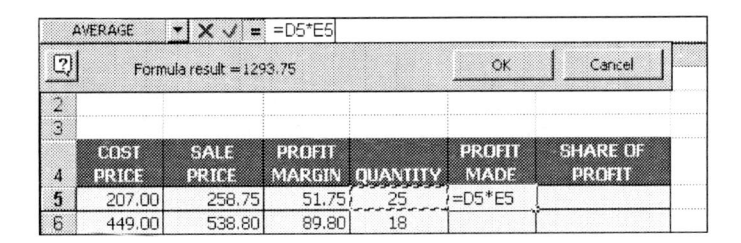

	AVERAGE	▼	X	✓	=	=D5*E5		
	❓	Formula result = 1293.75				OK	Cancel	
2								
3								
4	COST PRICE	SALE PRICE	PROFIT MARGIN	QUANTITY	PROFIT MADE	SHARE OF PROFIT		
5	207.00	258.75	51.75	25	=D5*E5			
6	449.00	538.80	89.80	18				

The formula result appears in the formula palette

- Click the **OK** button on the formula palette.

CALCULATIONS
Lesson 5.1: Formulas

> The formula palette makes it easier to insert a function into a calculation formula (cf. Lesson 5.2 - Functions).

2 ▪ Modifying formulas

- Double-click the cell containing the formulas you want to modify.

  The cell references that make up the formula appear in different colours. In the worksheet, a border of the same colour surrounds each cell or cell range existing in the formula.

- Modify the formula as required.
- Press ⏎ to confirm your modifications.

3 ▪ Using AutoSum

- Activate the cell that will display the result.
- Click the Σ tool or press Alt =.

	C	D	E	F	G
	AVERAGE	✕ ✓ =	=SUM(F5:F19)		
4	SALE PRICE	PROFIT MARGIN	QUANTITY	PROFIT MADE	SHARE OF PROFIT
5	258.75	51.75	25	1293.75	
6	538.80	89.80	18	1616.40	
7	238.80	39.80	42	1671.60	
8	518.70	119.70	58	6942.60	
9	58.50	13.50	57	769.50	
10	33.80	7.80	120	936.00	
11	183.30	42.30	14	592.20	
12	127.40	29.40	48	1411.20	
13	423.80	195.80	22	4307.60	
14	296.40	68.40	21	1436.40	
15	450.00	90.00	65	5850.00	
16	575.00	115.00	37	4255.00	
17	140.00	28.00	45	1260.00	
18	204.10	47.10	30	1413.00	
19	148.20	34.20	57	1949.40	
20				=SUM(F5:F19)	

Excel displays the integrated function called SUM and tries to guess which cells you want to add up.

- If you are not satisfied with this selection, use the mouse to change it.
- Confirm by pressing ↵.

4 ▪ Including absolute cell references in a formula

This technique is used to "fix" a cell reference and ensure it does not evolve when the formula is copied.
In the following example, the formula in cell G5 needs to be copied into cells G6 to G20. However, when you copy into cell G6, the formula will become =F6/F21...but cell F21 is empty! To obtain a correct result, the formula needs to be =F6/F20. You must make the reference of cell F20 absolute before copying the formula:

	AVERAGE	✗ ✓ =	=F5/F20	
	C	D	E	F	G
4	SALE PRICE	PROFIT MARGIN	QUANTITY	PROFIT MADE	SHARE OF PROFIT
5	258.75	51.75	25	1293.75	=F5/F20
6	538.80	89.80	18	1616.40	
7	238.80	39.80	42	1671.60	
8	518.70	119.70	58	6942.60	
9	58.50	13.50	57	769.50	
10	33.80	7.80	120	936.00	
11	183.30	42.30	14	592.20	
12	127.40	29.40	48	1411.20	
13	423.80	195.80	22	4307.60	
14	296.40	68.40	21	1436.40	
15	450.00	90.00	65	5850.00	
16	575.00	115.00	37	4255.00	
17	140.00	28.00	45	1260.00	
18	204.10	47.10	30	1413.00	
19	148.20	34.20	57	1949.40	
20				35704.65	
21					

CALCULATIONS
Lesson 5.1: Formulas

- Start entering the formula and stop after the cell reference that you want to make absolute. If you are modifying an existing formula, click the reference of the cell concerned.

- Press F4.

    The cell reference now contains $ signs before the column letter and before the row number:

	C	D	E	F	G
4	SALE PRICE	PROFIT MARGIN	QUANTITY	PROFIT MADE	SHARE OF PROFIT
5	258.75	51.75	25	1293.75	=F5/$F$20
6	538.80	89.80	18	1616.40	
7	238.80	39.80	42	1671.60	
8	518.70	119.70	58	6942.60	
9	58.50	13.50	57	769.50	
10	33.80	7.80	120	936.00	
11	183.30	42.30	14	592.20	
12	127.40	29.40	48	1411.20	
13	423.80	195.80	22	4307.60	
14	296.40	68.40	21	1436.40	
15	450.00	90.00	65	5850.00	
16	575.00	115.00	37	4255.00	
17	140.00	28.00	45	1260.00	
18	204.10	47.10	30	1413.00	
19	148.20	34.20	57	1949.40	
20				35704.65	
21					

    (Formula bar: AVERAGE = =F5/$F$20)

- Complete the formula if necessary then enter.

    When you press F4, you obtain an absolute cell reference; press F4 again and only the row reference remains absolute; if you press F4 a third time, it is the column reference that is absolute.

MOUS
Excel 2000 Core

Below you can see **Practice Exercise** 5.1. This exercise is made up of 4 steps. If you do not know how to complete one of the steps, go back to the lesson to refer to the corresponding title. When you have finished, check your work by reading the **Solution** on the next page.

All the steps in this exercise are likely to be tested in the exam.

☞ Practice Exercise 5.1

In order to complete exercise 5.1, you should open the **5-1 Furniture.xls** workbook in the **MOUS Excel 2000** folder then, if necessary, activate **Sheet1**.

1. In cell **F5**, enter a formula that will multiply the **Profit Margin** by the **Quantity**. Next, copy the contents of cell **F5** into the adjacent cells **F6** to **F19**.

2. In cell **D13**, the margin made by the product **Rectangular table** is wrong. The formula subtracts the Cost Price of the Wardrobe 2 door article from the Sale Price of the Rectangular table.
   You should modify the formula in cell **D13** so the Cost Price for the Rectangular table is subtracted from the Sale Price of the Rectangular table.

3. Find the total **Profit Made** and show the result in **F20**. Use the AutoSum function to do this.

CALCULATIONS
Exercise 5.1: Formulas

4. In cell **G5**, calculate the share of profit made by the Sofa Bed, taking into account the fact that this formula must then be copied into cells **G6** to **G20**; to calculate the share of the profit made by an article, divide the article's profit by the total profit made.

If you want to put what you have learnt into practice on a real document, you can work on summary exercise 5 for the CALCULATIONS section, that you can find at the end of this book.

MOUS
Excel 2000 Core

It is often possible to perform a task in several different ways, but here only the quickest solution is presented. Go back to the lesson to see the other techniques that can be used.

Solution to Exercise 5.1

1. To enter a formula that will multiply the Profit Made by the Quantity in cell **F5**, click cell **F5**.
   Type a = sign, click cell **D5**, type a * sign then click cell **E5**.
   Press the ⏎ key to enter the formula.

   To copy the contents of cell F5 onto cells F6 to F19, click in cell **F5**.
   Point to the fill handle on cell **F5**, then drag it down to cell **F19**.

2. To alter the formula in cell D13 to subtract the Cost Price of the Rectangular table from the Sale Price of the same product, double-click cell **D13** then delete the reference to cell **B14**.
   Click cell **B13** to add the **B13** cell reference to the formula then confirm your changes by pressing ⏎.

3. To calculate the total Profit Made in cell F20 using AutoSum, click cell **F20**.
   Click the Σ tool then press the ⏎ key to confirm.

4. To calculate the Share of profit made by the Sofa beds in cell G5, click cell **G5**.
   Type =, click cell **F5**, press the **/** key, click cell **F20** then press the F4 key.
   Press ⏎ to confirm your entry.

   To copy the formula in cell G5 into cells G6 to G20, click cell **G5**.
   Point to the fill handle on cell **G5**, and drag it down to cell **G20**.

CALCULATIONS
Exercise 5.1: Formulas

CALCULATIONS
Lesson 5.2: Functions

- 1 ▪ Using simple statistical functions 116
- 2 ▪ Using the IF function 116
- 3 ▪ Pasting a function 118
- 4 ▪ Using the formula palette to insert a function 119
- 5 ▪ Inserting the control date in a cell 121
- 6 ▪ Using financial functions 121

Practice Exercise 5.2 124

CALCULATIONS
Lesson 5.2: Functions

1 • Using simple statistical functions

- Select the cell that will contain the result.
- Type = followed by the name of one of the following common functions:

AVERAGE	to calculate the average value of a group of cells.
SUM	to calculate the sum of a group of cells.
COUNT	to count how many cells in a selected group contain numbers.
COUNTA	to count how many cells within a given group are not blank.
MAX	to extract the maximum value from a given group of cells.
MIN	to extract the minimum value from a given group of cells.

- Type an opening bracket (.
- Drag to select the cell range involved in the calculation. To select several cell ranges, select the first range, hold down the Ctrl key then select the other range(s); in the formula, the various cell ranges are separated by a comma (for example: =AVERAGE(A10:A20,C10:C20)).
- Type the closing bracket).
- Press the ↵ key to confirm the formula.

2 • Using the IF function

The IF logical function is used to obtain a result by setting one or more conditions.

- Activate the cell that will display the result.
- Set your condition, respecting the following syntax:
  =IF(condition,action if TRUE,action if FALSE)

	D	E	F	G	H	I
3						
4						
5	COMPUTER	TOTAL	AVERAGE TURNOVER	PERCENTAGE OF TURNOVER	OBJECTIVE	COMMISSION
6	5000	8500	2833.33	7%	Below Objective	425
7	6000	9500	3166.67	8%	Below Objective	475
8	6500	8500	2833.33	7%	Below Objective	425
9	7000	13200	4400.00	11%	Above Objective	1320
10	4500	10500	3500.00	9%	Above Objective	1050
11	7000	10000	3333.33	9%	Above Objective	500
12	5000	11000	3666.67	9%	Above Objective	1100
13	2000	4300	1433.33	4%	Below Objective	215
14	5000	8500	2833.33	7%	Below Objective	425
15	4500	9500	3166.67	8%	Below Objective	475
16	4200	10200	3400.00	9%	Above Objective	1020
17	8000	13600	4533.33	12%	Above Objective	1360
18	64700	117300		100%		

Cell I6: `=IF(E6<=10000,E6*5%,E6*10%)`

If the total in cell E6 is less than 10000, an amount of 5% commission is calculated; if E6 equals or is greater than 10000, 10% commission will be calculated.

※ In a conditional formula, a variety of actions can be performed:

- Displaying a number: enter the number,

- Displaying a text: enter the text between quotation marks,

- Displaying the result of a calculation: enter the calculation formula,

- Displaying the contents of a cell: select the cell,

- Displaying zero: enter nothing,

- No display: type "".

※ For conditions, several operators are available:

>/<   greater than/less than,

<>   different from,

>=/<= greater than or equal to/less than or equal to.

CALCULATIONS
Lesson 5.2: Functions

> To set several conditions, use one of the following functions, depending on the desired result. If several conditions should be met simultaneously:
> **=IF(AND(cond1,cond2, ... ,condn),action to be carried out if all the conditions are satisfied,action to be carried out if any condition is not satisfied)**
> If at least one condition must be met:
> **=IF(OR(cond1,cond2, ...,condn),action to be carried out if at least one condition is satisfied,action to be carried out if no condition is satisfied)**
> If several conditions are nested (one in the other):
> **=IF(cond1,action if TRUE,IF(cond2,action if TRUE,IF(cond 3,action if TRUE,action if FALSE)))**

3 ▪ Pasting a function

- Click the cell that will show the result.
- **Insert - Function** or *fx* or [Shift][F3]
- Select a **Function category** in the corresponding list:

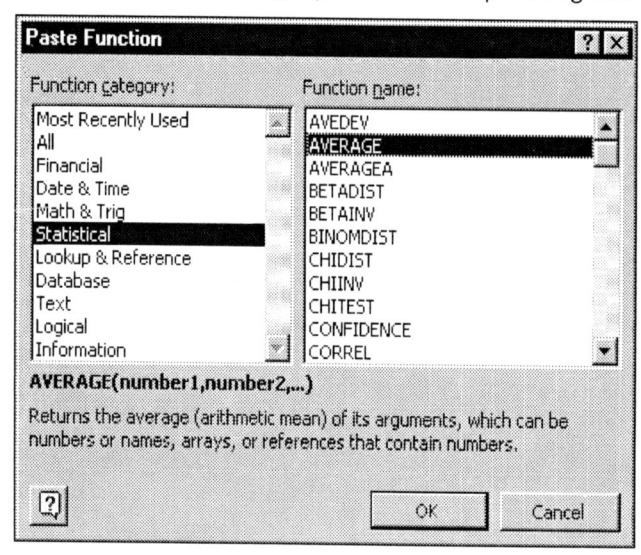

In the lower part of the dialog box, you can see the function's syntax as well as a description of what the function does.

The list of functions contained in each category appears on the right, in the **Function name** list. The **All** category shows a list of all the available functions within Excel.

* Click the required **Function name** in the corresponding list.
* Click **OK**.

The function and its arguments are displayed in the formula palette, which will assist you in creating the rest of the formula.

* To define each of the arguments in the function:

  - click in the corresponding text box then click the ▦ button,

  - on the worksheet, select the cell or cells corresponding to the argument,

  - click the ▦ button to expand the formula palette again.

* If necessary, complete the function then click **OK**.

You can see the formula result in the cell, while the calculation formula appears on the formula bar.

4 ▪ Using the formula palette to insert a function

* Click the cell that will contain the result.
* Click the ▦ button on the formula bar.

The formula palette is made up of the formula bar and the grey area containing the **OK** and **Cancel** buttons.

* Select a function from the first list on the formula palette (use the **More Functions** option if the desired function does not appear in the list).

CALCULATIONS
Lesson 5.2: Functions

* To define each argument in the function:

    - click in the corresponding text box then click the ![button] button,

    - on the worksheet, select the cell(s) corresponding to the argument,

    - click ![button] to expand the formula palette.

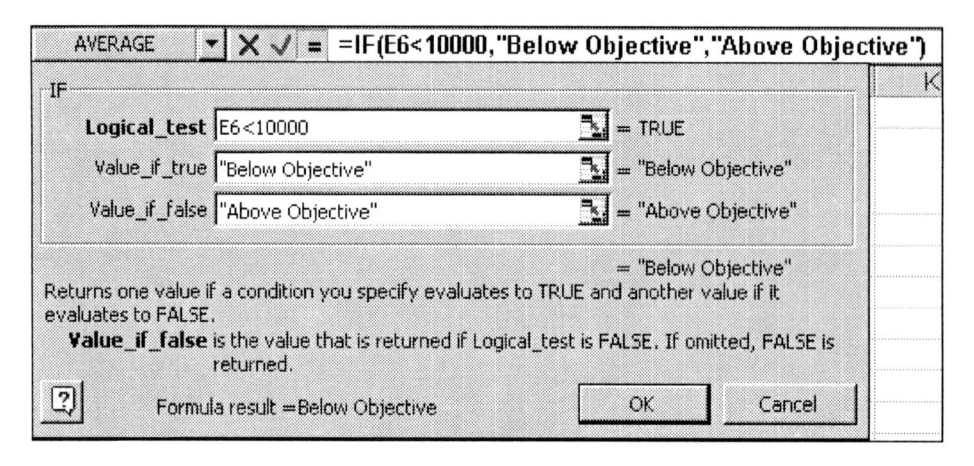

![IF function dialog box showing Logical_test E6<10000, Value_if_true "Below Objective", Value_if_false "Above Objective", with Formula result = Below Objective]

* If necessary, complete the formula then click **OK**.

    > The [Shift][F3] shortcut key opens the **Paste Function** dialog box that allows you to select a function from one of several categories.
    > You can also insert a formula by using the **Insert - Function** command.

MOUS
Excel 2000 Core

5 ▪ Inserting the control date in a cell

- Activate the cell where you want to display the date.
- Choose which of the three control dates you want to insert:

  =TODAY()   Computer's control date, automatically updated on opening the worksheet.

  =NOW()   Control date and time, updated whenever the worksheet is opened.

  [Ctrl][;] Control date, not automatically updated.

- Confirm by pressing ↵.

  > If the date shown is not correct, correct your computer's control date in the Windows' Control Panel.

6 ▪ Using financial functions

The FV financial function

This function calculates the future value of an investment, based on constant, regular payments and a stable interest rate.

- Click the cell that will display the result.
- Enter the calculation, respecting the following syntax:

  = FV (rate,nper,pmt,pv,type)

  In the function syntax, replace:

  rate   by the interest rate per period.
  nper   by the total number of repayments.
  pmt   by the total repayment value for each period.

CALCULATIONS
Lesson 5.2: Functions

pv by the present value, or the sum that the total repayments represent today.

type by the number specifying when each payment is due: 1 stands for the start of each period, 0 for the end of it.

The **pv** and **type** arguments are optional. If they are omitted, a default value of 0 (zero) is taken into account.

* Confirm by pressing ⏎.

A negative value is displayed. If you want Excel to show a positive value, put a - (minus) sign in front of the function name: **= -FV( )**.

The PMT financial function

This function calculates the interest payment on a loan based on constant periodic payments and a stable interest rate.

* Click the cell that will show the result.
* Enter your calculation, respecting the following syntax:

= PMT (rate,nper,pv,fv,type)

rate the interest rate.

nper the total number of repayments.

pv the current value of the sum borrowed.

fv the goal result you would like to obtain after the last payment (the future balance).

type the number that indicates when repayments should be made: 1 for the start of the period and 0 for the end.

The **fv** and **type** arguments are optional. If they are omitted, a default value of 0 (zero) is taken into account.

* Confirm by pressing ⏎.

If you want Excel to show a positive value, place a - sign in front of the function name: **=-PMT()**.

> It is important to use the same unit for the rate and nper arguments: if you make monthly repayments on a loan over a period of 5 years at an annual interest rate of 6%, use 6%/12 for the rate and 5*12 for nper. If the repayments are annual, you can use 6% for the rate and 5 for nper.

> If you use the formula palette to construct your formula (cf. Lesson 5.2 – 4. Using the formula palette to insert a function) you obtain a description of each argument as well as the calculation result in the bottom part of the window.

CALCULATIONS
Exercise 5.2: Functions

Below you can see **Practice Exercise** 5.2. This exercise is made up of 6 steps. If you do not know how to complete one of the steps, go back to the lesson to refer to the corresponding title. When you have finished, check your work by reading the **Solution** on the next page.

All the steps in this exercise are likely to be tested in the exam.

👉 Practice Exercise 5.2

1. In **Sheet1** of the **5-2 Furniture** workbook, in the **MOUS Excel 2000** folder, use common statistical functions to perform the following tasks:
   - calculate the total quantity of orders in cell **E20**.
   - calculate the number of products listed in cell **B22**.
   - calculate the average margin made in cell **B23**.
   - extract the best profit made into cell **B24**.
   - extract the worst profit made into cell **B25**.

2. Set a condition in cell **I6** of **Sheet1** in the **5-2 Hi-Fi.xls**, workbook to calculate a 5% commission on the Monthly Total, if this amount is less than or equal to 10000 or a 10% commission on the Monthly Total, if this amount is greater than 10000. Copy this formula into cells **I7** to **I17**.

3. Use the **Paste Function** dialog box to calculate the average Monthly Turnover for January in cell **F6** of **Sheet1** in the **5-2 Hi-Fi.xls** workbook. Copy this formula for the months February to December.

4. Using the formula palette, set a condition in cell **H6** of **Sheet1** in the **5-2 Hi-Fi.xls** workbook so it displays the text **Below Objective** if the total for January is less than 10000. If the January total is greater than or equal to 10000, the text **Above Objective** should be displayed.
Copy this formula into cells **H7** to **H17**.

5. In cell **B24** of **Sheet1** on the **5-2 Hi-Fi.xls** workbook, insert your computer's control date. This date should remain the same, and not be updated from day to day.

6. In cell **C16** of the **Taylor** worksheet in the **5-2 Loan.xls** workbook, calculate the total cost of the loan by using the **FV** financial function. The end result displayed should be in positive figures.

If you want to put what you have learnt into practice on a real document, you can work on summary exercise 5 for the CALCULATIONS section, that you can find at the end of this book.

CALCULATIONS
Exercise 5.2: Functions

It is often possible to perform a task in several different ways, but here only the quickest solution is presented. Go back to the lesson to see the other techniques that can be used.

Solution to Exercise 5.2

1. Open the **5-2 Furniture.xls** worksheet in the **MOUS Excel 2000** folder and click the **Sheet1** tab if necessary. To calculate the total order quantity in cell E20, start by clicking cell **E20**.
   Type **=sum(**
   select cells **E5** to **E19**
   type **)** then confirm by pressing ⏎.

   To calculate the total number of products in B22, click cell **B22**.
   Type **=counta(**
   select cells **B5** to **B19**
   type **)** then confirm by pressing ⏎.

   To calculate the average margin made in cell B23, click cell **B23**.
   Type **=average(**
   select cells **D5** to **D19**
   type **)** then confirm by pressing ⏎.

   To extract the best profit made and display the result in cell **B24**, click cell **B24**.
   Type **=max(**
   select cells **F5** to **F19**
   type **)** then confirm by pressing ⏎.

   To extract the lowest profit made and display the result in cell B25, click cell **B25**.
   Type **=min(**
   select cells **F5** to **F19**
   type **)** then confirm by pressing ⏎.

MOUS
Excel 2000 Core

2. Open the **5-2 Hi-Fi.xls** workbook in the **MOUS Excel 2000** folder then click the **Sheet1** tab if necessary.
   To set a condition in cell **I6** to calculate a commission of 5% on the Monthly Total if this sum is less than or equal to 10000 or a 10% commission if the total is greater than 10000, click cell **I6**.
   Type **=if(E6<=10000,E6*5%,E6*10%)** then confirm with ⏎.
   Copy this formula into cells **I7** to **I17** by drag the fill handle of cell **I6** down to cell **I17**.

3. To calculate the average turnover for January in cell **F6**, using the **Paste Function** dialog box, open the **5-2 Hi-Fi.xls** workbook in the **MOUS Excel 2000** folder, click the **Sheet1** tab then click cell **F6**.

   Use the **Insert - Function** command. Click the **Statistical** option in the **Function category** list then choose the **AVERAGE** function in the **Function name** list. Click **OK**.

   Click the button on the **Number 1** text box, select cells **B6** to **D6**, click the button then **OK**.

   Copy this formula into cells **F7** to **F17** by dragging the fill handle from cell **F6**.

4. To set a condition in cell H6, using the formula palette, in order to display the text **Below Objective** if the January Monthly Total is less than 10000 or the text **Above Objective** is the figure is greater than or equal to 10000, click the **Sheet1** tab on the **5-2 Hi-Fi.xls** workbook then click cell **H6**.

   Click the button on the formula bar.
   Open the first list on the formula bar then click the **IF** function.

   Click the button on the **Logical_test** text box, select cell **E6**, type a < sign followed by **10000** then click the button.
   Click the **Value_if_true** box then type **Below Objective.**
   Click the **Value_if_false** box and type **Above Objective.**
   Confirm your formula by clicking **OK**.

   Copy it by dragging the fill handle on cell **H6** down over cells **H7** to **H17**.

CALCULATIONS
Exercise 5.2: Functions

5. To insert a non-updated control date in cell **B24**, click cell **B24** in **Sheet1**, type [Ctrl] [:] and confirm with [↵].

6. To calculate the total cost of the loan in cell **C16** on the **Taylor** worksheet in the **5-2 Loan.xls** workbook, open the **5-2 Loan.xls** workbook, click the **Taylor** tab then click cell **C16**.

Type =**-FV(C11/C12,C12,C14)** and confirm by pressing [↵].

PRESENTATION OF DATA
Lesson 6.1: Formatting data

1 ▪ Modifying font and/or size of characters 130

2 ▪ Modifying font colour 131

3 ▪ Modifying text attributes 131

4 ▪ Formatting numerical values 133

5 ▪ Modifying the number of decimal places 134

6 ▪ Formatting dates 135

7 ▪ Modifying the horizontal alignment of cell contents 135

8 ▪ Aligning cell contents vertically 136

9 ▪ Copying formats 136

10 ▪ Applying an AutoFormat to a table 137

11 ▪ Modifying cell borders 148

12 ▪ Applying colour to the background of cells 140

13 ▪ Applying a pattern to the background of cells 140

14 ▪ Merging cells 142

15 ▪ Modifying the orientation of text 143

16 ▪ Indenting text in a cell 144

Practice Exercise 6.1 145

PRESENTATION OF DATA
Lesson 6.1: Formatting data

1 ▪ Modifying font and/or size of characters

- Select the cells or data concerned. If you wish to select only some of the characters contained in a cell, select those characters in the formula bar.

- Select the font and font size in the first two list boxes on the **Formatting** toolbar:

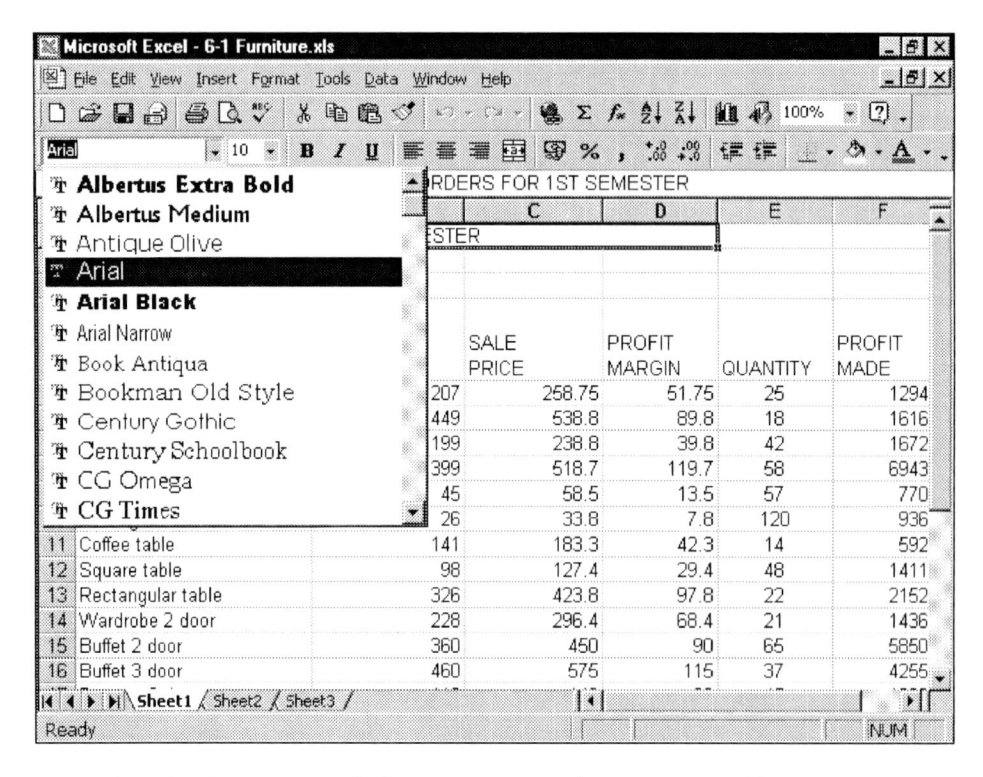

Fonts that display a TT symbol are True Type fonts managed by Windows.

- To define the default font and font size for any new workbook, use **Tools - Options - General** tab (**Standard font** and **Size** options). These changes will only take effect when you restart Excel.

*You can also use the **Format - Font** command to change the font or font size used.*

2 ▪ Modifying font colour

- Select the cells or data concerned.
- Open the drop-down list on the [A▼] tool on the **Formatting** toolbar, by clicking the black triangle.
- Click the colour you wish to use.

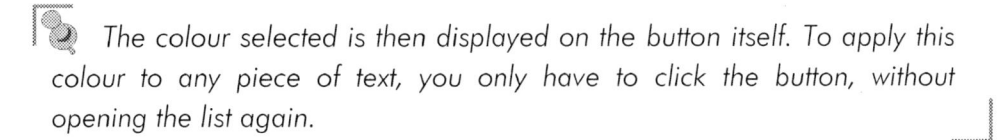

The colour selected is then displayed on the button itself. To apply this colour to any piece of text, you only have to click the button, without opening the list again.

- Select the cells or data concerned.
- **Format - Cells** or [Ctrl] 1
- Click the **Font** tab.
- Open the list on the **Colour** option then click the required colour.
- Click **OK**.

3 ▪ Modifying text attributes

- Select the cells or data concerned.
- Choose between:
    [B] or [Ctrl] B to apply a **bold** typeface.

PRESENTATION OF DATA
Lesson 6.1: Formatting data

I or `Ctrl` **I** to apply *italics*.

U or `Ctrl` **U** to apply underlining.

> If you repeat the same command for the same text, you cancel the corresponding attribute.
> You can apply more than one attribute to the same text.

* Select the cells or data concerned.
* **Format - Cells** or `Ctrl` **1**
* Click the **Font** tab.
* Activate all the formats to be applied to the text.

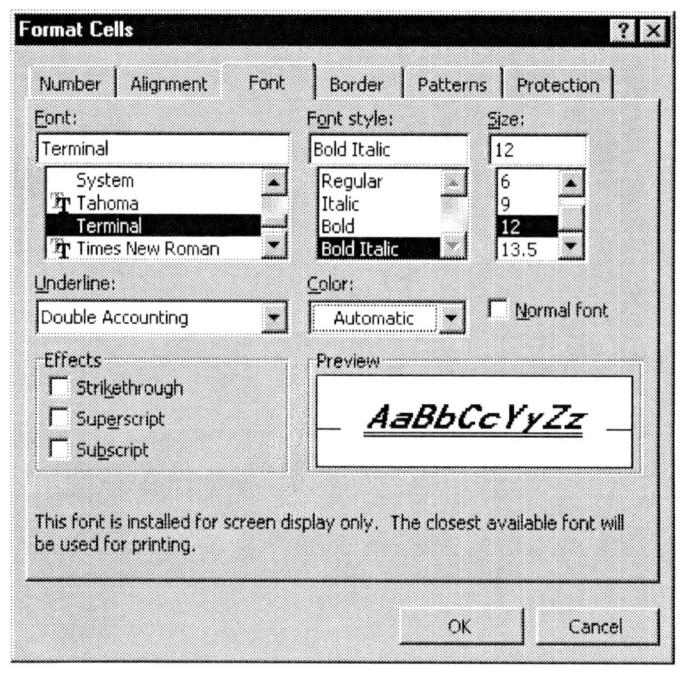

*The three options in the **Effects** frame and some of the **Underline** options are all options that are only available through the menus.*

* Click **OK**.

4 ▪ Formatting numerical values

- Select the values concerned.
- Choose one of the following formats:

🔲	Currency	(£10,000.00 or $10,000.00, depending on your Regional Settings)
🔲	Euro	(10 000,00 €)
🔲	Percent	(100 000%)
🔲	Comma	(10,000.00)

- Select the values concerned.
  - **Format - Cells**
  - Click the **Number** tab.
  - Use the **Category** list to select the format category you wish to use.

PRESENTATION OF DATA
Lesson 6.1: Formatting data

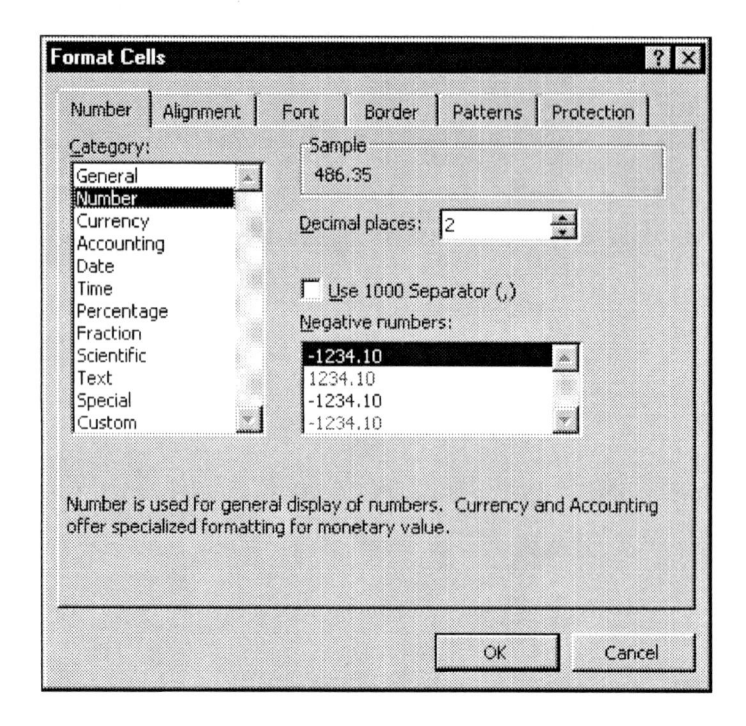

- If necessary, modify the format parameters; for example, specify the number of decimal places to be used.
- Click **OK**.

> Hash symbols may appear in some cells if the column width is insufficient to display the requested format.

5 ▪ Modifying the number of decimal places

- Select the values concerned.
- To add a decimal place, click the tool.
- To delete a decimal place, click the tool.

> *You can also use the **Format - Cells** command to define the number of decimal places to be displayed.*

6 ▪ Formatting dates

- Select the dates you wish to format.
- **Format - Cells** or `Ctrl` **1**
- If necessary, activate the **Number** tab.
- Select the **Date** format type in the **Category** list, if it is not already active.
- Select the desired format in the **Type** list.
- Click **OK**.

7 ▪ Modifying the horizontal alignment of cell contents

Horizontal alignment is calculated according to the width of each column.

- Select the cells concerned.
- Click one of the following three tools:

  align on the left

  centre

  align on the right

- Select the cells concerned.
- **Format - Cells** or `Ctrl` **1**
- Click the **Alignment** tab.
- Select the required alignment from the **Horizontal** list box.

PRESENTATION OF DATA
Lesson 6.1: Formatting data

- To indent contents within a cell, give the indent to apply to the left edge of the cell in the **Indent** box.
- Click **OK**.

8 • Aligning cell contents vertically

Vertical alignment is defined with reference to the row height.

- Select the cells concerned.
- **Format - Cells** or `Ctrl` 1
- Click the **Alignment** tab.
- Select the required alignment from the **Vertical** list box.
- Click **OK**.

9 • Copying formats

This technique copies the presentation of one cell range onto another.

- Select the cell(s) containing the format you want to copy.
- Click the ✏ tool.

The pointer takes the form of a paintbrush.

- Select the cells that are to take the copied format.

> If you wish to copy the format onto several different places, select the ✏ tool with a double-click. Press `Esc` to deactivate the format painter.

MOUS
Excel 2000 Core

10 ▪ Applying an AutoFormat to a table

- Select the table you wish to format.
- **Format - AutoFormat**
- In the list of AutoFormats, choose the most suitable style.

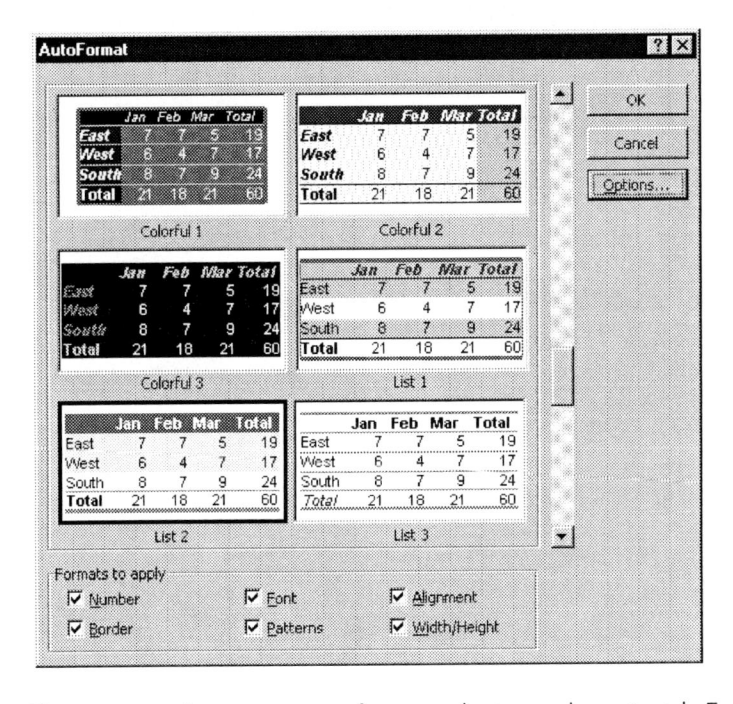

Excel shows a sample list of the various formats that can be applied.

- If necessary deactivate any formats that you do not wish Excel to apply.
- Click **OK**.

11 ▪ Modifying cell borders

- Select the cells concerned.
- Open the 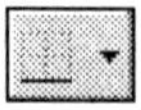 list by clicking the black triangle.

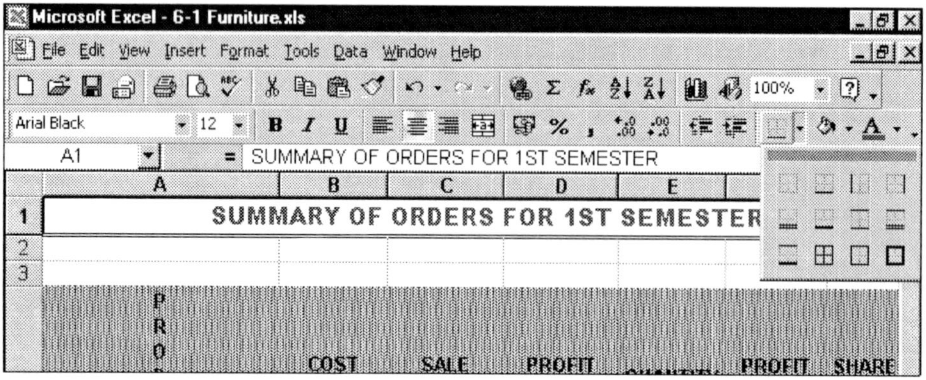
Microsoft Excel - 6-1 Furniture.xls
File Edit View Insert Format Tools Data Window Help
100%
Arial Black
12
A1
SUMMARY OF ORDERS FOR 1ST SEMESTER
A
B
C
D
E
SUMMARY OF ORDERS FOR 1ST SEMESTER
COST
SALE
PROFIT
PROFIT
SHARE

- Click the required style of border.

The 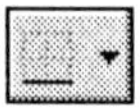 tool now shows a picture of the last border style chosen.

- Deselect to see the new border more clearly.

To apply coloured or noncontinuous borders, you must use the menu options.

To remove all borders, click the  button.

To apply the same border to another selection of cells, you can click the tool button without opening the list.

MOUS
Excel 2000 Core

- Select the cells concerned.
- **Format - Cells** or **Ctrl 1**
- Click the **Border** tab.
- To put a border all around the edge of the selection, choose the **Style** and **Color** of the border then click the **Outline** button.
- To place a border along one or more edges of the selection, choose first a **Style** and **Color** then in the **Border** frame, click the buttons corresponding to the borders you wish to display or hide. Click the **Inside** button to apply the border to the edges of each individual cell in the selection.

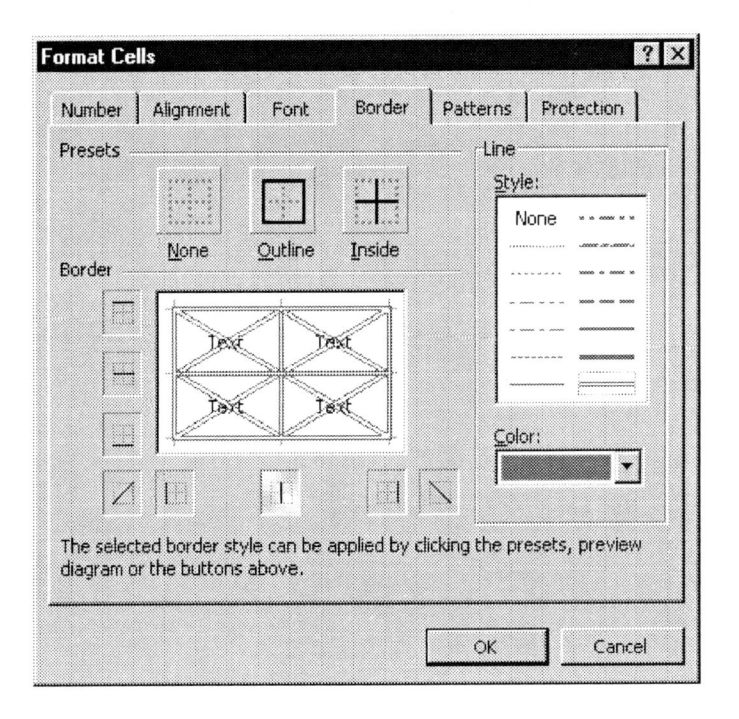

The ◸ and ◹ buttons are used to draw diagonal lines through cells.

- Confirm by clicking **OK**.
- Show the result by clicking outside the selected cells.

PRESENTATION OF DATA
Lesson 6.1: Formatting data

12 ▪ Applying colour to the background of a cell

- Select the cells you wish to colour.
- Open the [icon] list by clicking the black triangle.
- Click the required colour.

    The [icon] tool shows the last colour chosen. Click this button (*without opening the list*) to apply this same colour to other selected cells.

- Click outside the selection to see the results clearly.

    📄 You can also use the **Color** list on the **Patterns** tab of the **Format Cells** dialog box (**Format - Cells**) to change the colour of cells.

13 ▪ Applying a pattern to the background of a cell

- Select the cells concerned.
- **Format - Cells** or [Ctrl] 1
- Click the **Patterns** tab.
- If necessary, choose a **Color** for the cell background.
- Open the **Pattern** list to choose a pattern type and a pattern colour.

MOUS
Excel 2000 Core

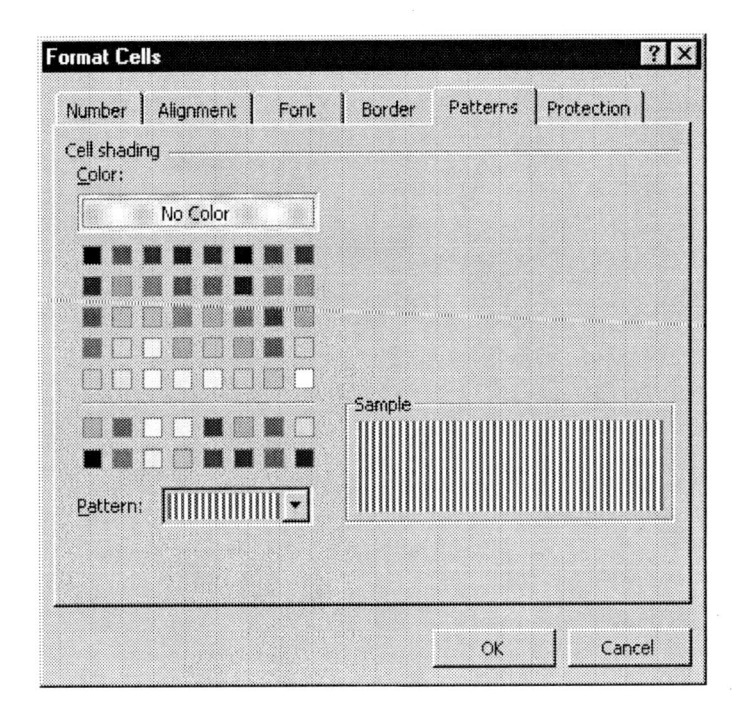

- Click **OK**.
- Show the result by clicking outside the selected cells.

PRESENTATION OF DATA
Lesson 6.1: Formatting data

14 ▪ Merging cells

Cells that have been merged become a single cell:

	A	B	C	D
1	SUMMARY OF ORDERS FOR 15 APRIL			
2				
3				
4			Quantity	Unit Price
5	PRODUCTS	Sofas	3	269
6		Tables	5	79
7		Chairs	12	46
8		Wardrobes	4	189
9		Beds	3	498
10		Total	27	1081

The text PRODUCTS belongs to cell A5 but appears over cells A5, A6, A7, A8 and A9, which are merged.

* Select the cells concerned.

  Only the data in the first cell of the selection (at the top left of the range of cells) will appear in the merged cells.

* **Format - Cells** or Ctrl 1

* Click the **Alignment** tab.

* Activate the **Merge cells** option.

* If necessary, specify the **Text alignment** that you wish to apply to the data in the merged cells.

* Click **OK**.

  The button merges selected cells (provided that they are in the same row) and centres the data in the first cell across the merged cells.

MOUS
Excel 2000 Core

15 ▪ Modifying the orientation of text

- Select the cells concerned.
- **Format - Cells** or `Ctrl` **1**
- Click the **Alignment** tab.

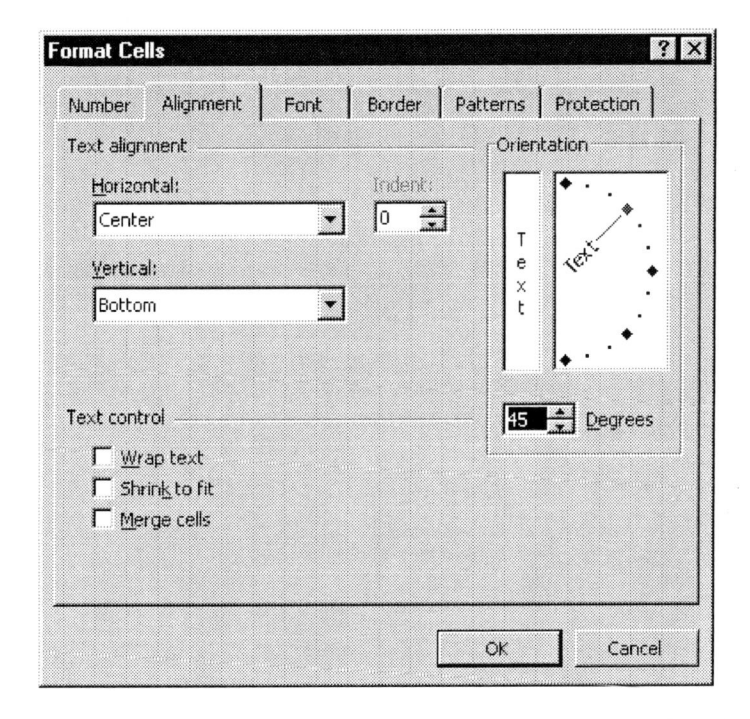

- In the **Orientation** frame, drag the horizontal word **Text** to define the rotation angle. You can also define this angle by changing the value in the **Degrees** box.
- Click **OK**.

  *To position characters one underneath the other, click the box in the **Orientation** frame where the word **Text** appears vertically.*

PRESENTATION OF DATA
Lesson 6.1: Formatting data

16 ▪ Indenting text in a cell

- Select the cells concerned.
- **Format - Cells** or Ctrl 1
- Click the **Alignment** tab.
- In the **Horizontal** list, select the **Left (Indent)** option.
- In the **Indent** text box, select or enter the indent value required (expressed as a number of characters).
- Click **OK**.

> You can also indent text in a cell by clicking the ⬚ tool to decrease the indent by one character or the ⬚ tool to increase the indent by one character.

MOUS
Excel 2000 Core

Below you can see **Practice Exercise** 6.1. This exercise is made up of 16 steps. If you do not know how to complete one of the steps, go back to the lesson to refer to the corresponding title. When you have finished, check your work by reading the **Solution** on the next page.

All the steps in this exercise are likely to be tested in the exam.

☞ Practice Exercise 6.1

In order to complete exercise 6.1, you should open the **6-1 Furniture.xls** workbook located in the **MOUS Excel 2000** folder and activate, if necessary, **Sheet1**.

1. In cell **A1**, modify the character font to **Arial Black** and the font size to **12**.

2. Modify the colour of the characters in cell **A1** to **red**.

3. Make the following formatting changes:
   - Put cells **B4** to **G4** then cells **A22** to **A25** in **bold** type.
   - Put the characters in cell **A1** in italics.
   - Underline the characters in cell **A28**.

4. Apply a **Comma** style to cells **B5** to **D19**.

5. Delete two decimal places from cells **B5** to **D19**.

6. Format the date in cell **B28** in an **mmmm dd yyyy** format (for example: December 26, 2000).

7. Centre the contents of cells **B4** to **G4** horizontally.

PRESENTATION OF DATA
Lesson 6.1: Formatting data

8. Centre the contents of cells **B4** to **G4** vertically.

9. Copy the formatting of cell **B4** onto cell **A4**.

10. To cells **A22** to **B25** apply a **Classic 3** AutoFormat; the alignment and cell width and height should not be modified.

11. Put borders around cells **A4** to **G20** following the illustration below:

PRODUCT	COST PRICE	SALE PRICE	PROFIT MARGIN	QUANTITY	PROFIT MADE	SHARE OF PROFIT
Sofa bed	207	259	52	25	1294	4%
Sofa (3 seater)	449	539	90	18	1616	5%
Single bed	199	239	40	42	1672	5%
Double bed	399	519	120	58	6943	21%
Dining chair	45	59	14	57	770	2%
Folding chair	26	34	8	120	936	3%
Coffee table	141	183	42	14	592	2%
Square table	98	127	29	48	1411	4%
Rectangular table	326	424	98	22	2152	6%
Wardrobe 2 door	228	296	68	21	1436	4%
Buffet 2 door	360	450	90	65	5850	17%
Buffet 3 door	460	575	115	37	4255	13%
Dresser 3 drawers	112	140	28	45	1260	4%
Bookshelf large	157	204	47	30	1413	4%
Bookshelf small	114	148	34	57	1949	6%
TOTAL					33549	100%

12. Apply a **Gray - 25%** background colour to cells **A4** to **G4** and **A20** to **G20**.

13. Apply this pattern: to the background of cells **A4** to **G4** and **A20** to **G20**.

14. Merge cells **A1** to **G1** and, simultaneously, centre the content of **A1** across columns A to G.

15. Apply a **-90% Degrees** orientation to cell **A4**.

16. Apply a left indent, two characters wide, in cells **A5** to **A19**.

If you want to put what have learnt into practice on a real document, you can work on summary exercise 6 for the PRESENTATION OF DATA section that you can find at the end of this book.

PRESENTATION OF DATA
Lesson 6.1: Formatting data

It is often possible to perform a task in several different ways, but here only the quickest solution is presented. Go back to the lesson to see the other techniques that can be used.

Solution to Exercise 6.1

1. To modify the font in cell A1 to **Arial Black** and the font size to 12, click cell **A1**.
   Open the first list box on the **Formatting** toolbar then click the **Arial Black** font.
   Open the second list box on the **Formatting** toolbar then click a size of **12**.

2. To put the characters in cell A1 in red, click cell **A1**.
   Open the list on the [A▼] tool then click the red colour.

3. To put cells B4 to G4 then cells A22 to A25 in bold type, select cells **B4** to **G4** and hold down the [Ctrl] key and select cells **A22** to **A25**.
   Click the [B] tool.

   To put the characters in cell A1 in italics, click cell **A1** then click the [I] tool.

   To underline the characters in cell A28, click cell **A28** then the [U] tool.

4. To apply a Comma style to cells B5 to D19, select cells **B5** to **D19** then click the [,] tool.

5. To delete two decimal places from cells B5 to D19, select cells **B5** to **D19** then click the [.00→.0] tool twice.

MOUS
Excel 2000 Core

6. To put the date in cell B28 in a mmmm dd yyyy format, click cell **B28**, use the **Format - Cells** command then click the **Number** tab.
Select **Date** in the **Category** list then in the **Type** list, click **March 14, 1998**. Confirm by clicking **OK**.

7. To centre the contents of cells B4 to G4 horizontally, select cells **B4** to **G4** then click the [icon] tool..

8. To centre the contents of cells B4 to G4 vertically, select cells **B4** to **G4** and use the **Format - Cells** command. Click the **Alignment** tab.
Open the **Vertical** list box then click the **Center** option.
Click **OK** to confirm.

9. To copy the format of cell B4 to cell A4, select cell **B4**. Click the [icon] tool then click cell **A4**.

10. To apply a **Classic 3** AutoFormat to cells A22 to B25, without affecting the alignment or cell width/height, select cells **A22** to **B25**.
Use the **Format - AutoFormat** command then select the **Classic 3** format.
Click the **Options** button and deactivate the **Alignment** and **Width/Height** options then click **OK**.

11. To apply borders around cells A4 to G20, select cells **A4** to **G20**, open the list on the [icon] tool and click the [icon] border type.

    Select cells **A4** to **G4** and **A19** to **G19**, open the list on the [icon] tool then click the [icon] border type.
    Select cells **A4** to **G20**, use the **Format - Cells** command and click the **Border** tab. In the **Style** box, select the last line style in the first column, click the [icon] button in the **Border** frame then click **OK**.
    Click outside the selection to see the result.

149

PRESENTATION OF DATA
Lesson 6.1: Formatting data

12. To apply a Gray -25% colour to cells A4 to G4 and A20 to G20, select cells **A4** to **G4** and **A20** to **G20**.
    Open the list on the ![tool] tool and click the **Gray - 25%** colour.
    Click outside the selection to see the result.

13. To apply a ![pattern] pattern to cells A4 to G4 and A20 to G20, select cells **A4** to **G4** and **A20** to **G20**.
    Use the **Format - Cells** command then click the **Patterns** tab.
    Open the **Patterns** list, click the ![pattern] pattern style then click **OK**.
    Click outside the selection to see the result.

14. To merge and centre cells A1 to G1 simultaneously, select cells **A1** to **G1** then click the ![tool] tool.

15. To apply a -90 degrees orientation to the text in cell A4, click cell **A4** to select it, use the **Format - Cells** command then click the **Alignment** tab.
    Type **-90** in the **Degrees** box then click **OK**.

16. To make a two-character left indent in cells A5 to A19, select cells **A5** to **A19** then click the ![tool] tool twice.

PRESENTATION OF DATA
Lesson 6.2: Styles

- 1 ▪ Creating a style 152
- 2 ▪ Applying a style 153
- 3 ▪ Managing existing styles 153

Practice Exercise 6.2 154

PRESENTATION OF DATA
Lesson 6.2 : Styles

1 • Creating a style

Creating a style is a useful way of saving a certain group of attributes that you want to be able to apply quickly to other cells.

- Activate the cell whose formatting is to be saved as a style.
- **Format - Style** or `Alt '`
- Enter a new **Style name** for the style you are creating.

  *A description of the style is displayed in the **Style Includes (By Example)** frame.*

- Deactivate any attributes that you do not want to include in the style.

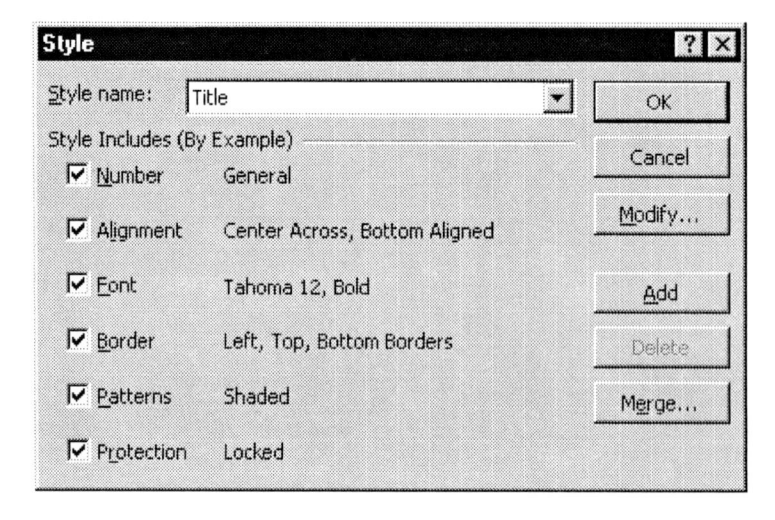

- If necessary, use the **Modify** button to change some of the style's attributes before saving it.
- Click **OK**.

2 ▪ Applying a style

- Select the cells to be formatted.
- **Format - Style** or [Alt]['].
- In the **Style name** list, select the style you want to use.
- Click **OK**.

3 ▪ Managing existing styles

Modifying a style

- **Format - Style** or [Alt]['].
- Select the style you want to modify in the **Style name** list.
- Click the **Modify** button.
- Make any changes then click **OK**.
- Click **OK** again.

Deleting a style

- **Format - Style** or [Alt]['].
- Select the **Style name** you want to delete then click the **Delete** button.
- Click **OK**.

PRESENTATION OF DATA
Exercise 6.2: Styles

Below you can see **Practice Exercise** 6.2. This exercise is made up of 3 steps. If you do not know how to complete one of the steps, go back to the lesson to refer to the corresponding title. When you have finished, check your work by reading the **Solution** on the next page.

All the steps in this exercise are likely to be tested in the exam.

☞ Practice Exercise 6.2

In order to complete exercise 6.2, you should open the **6-2 Sales Progression.xls** workbook located in the **MOUS Excel 2000** folder then activate the **Results** sheet if necessary.

1. Using the presentation of cell **A1** to help you, create a style called **Title**.

2. Apply the **Title** style to cell **A1** of the **Progression** worksheet.

3. Modify the **Title** style to include an indigo font colour.

If you want to put what have learnt into practice on a real document, you can work on summary exercise 6 for the PRESENTATION OF DATA section that you can find at the end of this book.

MOUS
Excel 2000 Core

It is often possible to perform a task in several different ways, but here only the quickest solution is presented. Go back to the lesson to see the other techniques that can be used.

Solution to Exercise 6.2

1. To create a **Title** style from the presentation of cell A1, click cell **A1** then use the **Format - Style** command.
   Type **Title** in the **Style name** box then click **OK**.

2. To apply the Title style to cell A1 on the Progression worksheet, click the **Progression** tab then cell **A1** and use the **Format - Style** command.
   Open the **Style name** list, select the **Title** style then click **OK**.

3. To add an indigo font colour to the Title style, use the **Format - Style** command.
   Select **Title** in the **Style name** list then click the **Modify** button.
   Click the **Font** tab and open the drop-down list on the **Color** option. Click the indigo colour.
   Click **OK** once, then click it again.

PRESENTATION OF DATA
Exercise 6.2: Styles

PRINTING
Lesson 7.1: Printing

1. Printing a worksheet 158
2. Printing a group of pages 158
3. Printing cells, sheets or a whole workbook 159
4. Printing several copies 160
5. Using Print Preview 160
6. Using Web Page Preview 162
7. Managing page breaks 163
8. Creating a print area 164

Practice Exercise 7.1 165

PRINTING
Lesson 7.1: Printing

1 ▪ Printing a worksheet

- Activate the sheet you want to print.
- Click the 🖨 tool.

    Excel gives you a brief opportunity to **Cancel** the print job; the data is then transmitted to Windows' Print Manager and the pages corresponding to the worksheet are printed.

2 ▪ Printing a group of pages

- Go to the sheet concerned.
- **File - Print** or `Ctrl` **P**
- Under **Print Range**, click the **From** box and enter the number of the first page to print then enter the number of the last page in the **To** box.

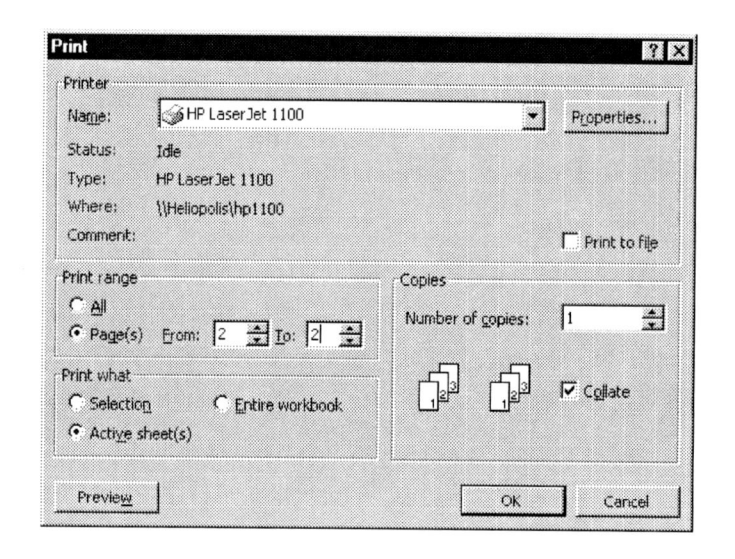

MOUS
Excel 2000 Core

- Click **OK**.

3 ▪ Printing cells, sheets or a whole workbook

Printing cells

- Select the cells you want to print.
- **File - Print** or `Ctrl` **P**
- Choose the **Selection** option under **Print what**.
- Click **OK**.

> 📄 You can also open the **Print** dialog box by clicking the **Print** button on the Print Preview page.

Printing sheets

- Select the sheets you want to print.
- **File - Print** or `Ctrl` **P**
- Choose the **Active sheet(s)** option in the **Print what** frame.
- Click **OK**.

Printing a whole workbook

- **File - Print** or `Ctrl` **P**
- Choose the **Entire workbook** option under **Print what**.
- Click **OK**.

PRINTING
Lesson 7.1: Printing

📖4 ▪ Printing several copies

- **File - Print** or `Ctrl` **P**
- Give the **Number of copies** you want to print in the corresponding text box.
- Click **OK**.

📖5 ▪ Using Print Preview

- **File - Print Preview** or 🔍

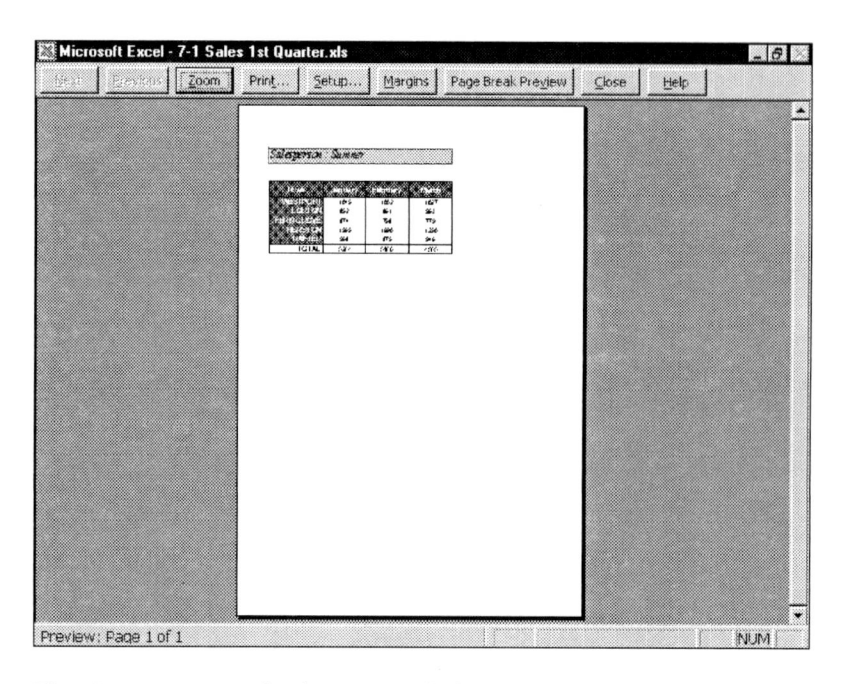

The Print Preview displays a scaled-down image of the sheet as it will appear when printed. On the status bar, Excel displays the current page number and the total number of sheets to be printed.

MOUS
Excel 2000 Core

- To zoom in on a preview, place the mouse pointer on the item to be magnified and click.

  Before you click, the pointer appears as a magnifying glass; once you have zoomed in on a detail, it appears as an arrow.

- To return to the scaled-down preview, click the page again.
- To display another page, use the **Next** and **Previous** buttons.

  In the scaled-down preview, you can also use the vertical scroll bars to change page.

- To modify margins and column widths, click the **Margins** button then drag the appropriate handle:

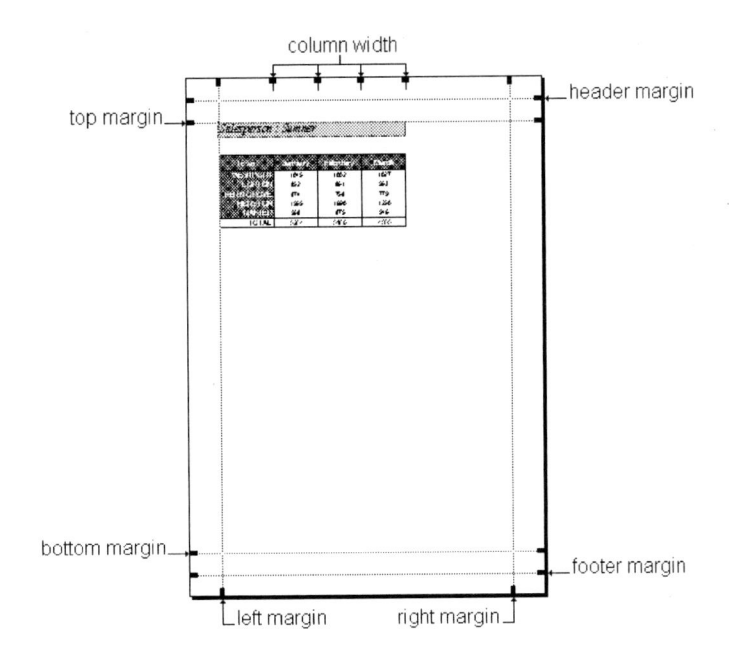

[Diagram showing a page preview with labels: column width, header margin, top margin, bottom margin, footer margin, left margin, right margin]

- To start printing, click the **Print** button, check the printing options are correct then enter.
- To leave Print Preview, click the **Close** button or press [Esc].

161

PRINTING

Lesson 7.1: Printing

> The **Page Break Preview** button makes the page breaks visible so you can reposition them if required.

6 ▪ Using Web Page Preview

- Open the Web page you want to view (htm format) in Excel as you would with any other workbook.

- **File - Web Page Preview**

  The default browser opens and the Web page appears as it would be seen on the Internet or an intranet network.

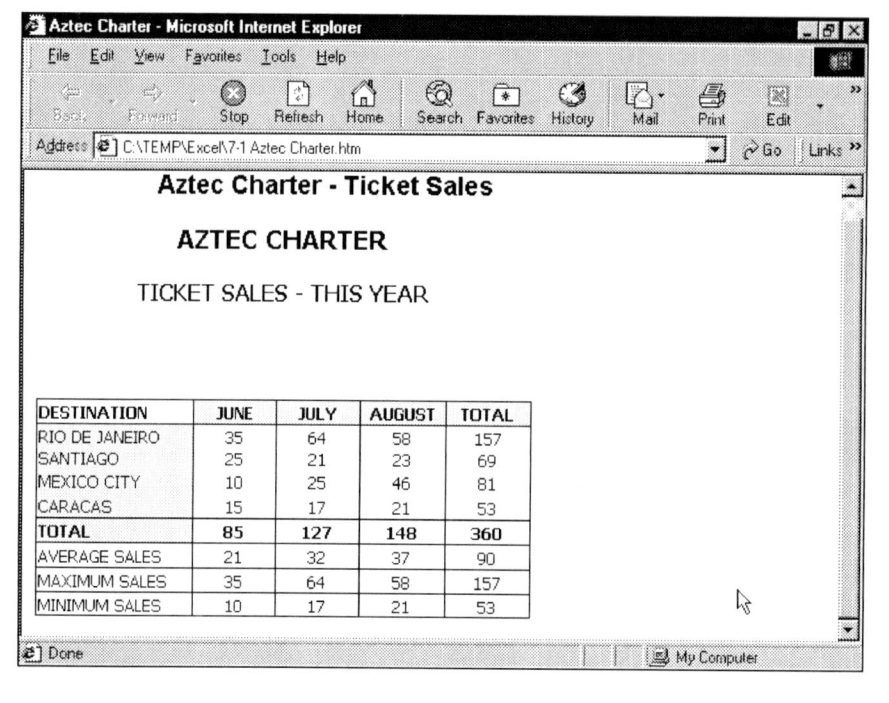

DESTINATION	JUNE	JULY	AUGUST	TOTAL
RIO DE JANEIRO	35	64	58	157
SANTIAGO	25	21	23	69
MEXICO CITY	10	25	46	81
CARACAS	15	17	21	53
TOTAL	85	127	148	360
AVERAGE SALES	21	32	37	90
MAXIMUM SALES	35	64	58	157
MINIMUM SALES	10	17	21	53

In this example, Internet Explorer 5 is the default browser used..

- Close the browser when you have finished viewing the page.

The Excel window reappears.

Managing page breaks

Inserting a page break

- Activate the cell which will be the first of your new page.

  The page break will be inserted above and to the left of the active cell.

- **Insert - Page Break**

  Almost instantly, a dotted line appears representing the page break.

  *To delete this type of page break, activate a cell in the next row or column and use **Insert - Remove Page Break**.*

Managing existing page breaks

- **View - Page Break Preview**

  *This option is also available in Print Preview: click the **Page Break Preview** button.*

- A dialog box may appear, informing you that you can drag page breaks to move them. If you do not want this dialog box to appear again, activate the **Do not show this dialog again** option then click **OK**.

PRINTING

Lesson 7.1: Printing

Page breaks are represented by blue lines on the worksheet. These lines do not prevent you from working normally (entering and editing data, changing the way it is presented…).

- To move a page break, drag the blue line into a new position.
- To return to the usual view of the page, use the **View - Normal** command.

▫ Creating a print area

A print area corresponds to a defined part of a sheet that you wish to print.

- Select the area you wish to print.
- **File - Print Area - Set Print Area**

To delete the print area, use **File - Print Area - Clear Print Area**.

MOUS
Excel 2000 Core

Below you can see **Practice Exercise** 7.1. This exercise is made up of 8 steps. If you do not know how to complete one of the steps, go back to the lesson to refer to the corresponding title. When you have finished, check your work by reading the **Solution** on the next page.

All the steps in this exercise are likely to be tested in the exam.

👉 Practice Exercise 7.1

1. Print the **Sumner** worksheet from the **7-1 Sales 1st Quarter.xls** workbook in the **MOUS Excel 2000** folder

2. Print page two of the **Base** sheet in the **7-1 Sport Base.xls** workbook in the **MOUS Excel 2000** folder.

3. Print cells **A22** to **B25** from the **Sheet1** worksheet in the **7-1 Furniture.xls** workbook in the **MOUS Excel 2000** folder.

4. Print three copies of the **Sheet1** worksheet in the **7-1 Furniture.xls** workbook in the **MOUS Excel 2000** folder.

5. Go into Print Preview for the **Sumner** worksheet in the **7-1 Sales 1st Quarter** workbook, located in the **MOUS Excel 2000** folder. Use the **Margins** button to set the top margin to **5 cm** (or about 2 inches).

6. Go into Web Page Preview for the **7-1 Aztec Charter.htm** Web page located in the **MOUS Excel 2000** folder.

7. Insert a page break between rows **13** and **14** on **Sheet1** of the **7-1 Furniture.xls** workbook in the **MOUS Excel 2000** folder.

PRINTING
Exercise 7.1: Printing

8. Create a print area that takes in cells **A5** to **E18** on **Sheet1** of the **7-1 Hi-Fi.xls** workbook in the **MOUS Excel 2000** folder.

If you want to put what have learnt into practice on a real document, you can work on summary exercise 7 for the PRINTING section that you can find at the end of this book.

MOUS
Excel 2000 Core

It is often possible to perform a task in several different ways, but here only the quickest solution is presented. Go back to the lesson to see the other techniques that can be used.

Solution to Exercise 7.1

1. To print the Sumner worksheet in the **7-1 Sales 1st Quarter.xls** workbook, open the **7-1 Sales 1st Quarter.xls** workbook in the **MOUS Excel 2000** folder, click the **Sumner** tab then the 🖨 tool.

2. To print page two of the Base sheet in the **7-1 Sport Base.xls** workbook, open the **7-1 Sport Base.xls** workbook in the **MOUS Excel 2000** folder then use the **File - Print** command.
Under **Print range** click the **From** box and enter **2**, then click the **To** box and enter **2**.
Click **OK**.

3. To print cells A22 to B25 on Sheet1 of the **7-1 Furniture.xls** workbook, open the **7-1 Furniture.xls** workbook in the **MOUS Excel 2000** folder then click the **Sheet1** tab.
Select cells **A22** to **B25** then use the **File - Print** command.
Click the **Selection** option in the **Print what** frame then click **OK**.

4. To print three copies of Sheet1 of the **7-1 Furniture.xls** workbook, open the **7-1 Furniture.xls** workbook in the **MOUS Excel 2000** folder.
Click the **Sheet1** tab then use the **File - Print** command.
Enter **3** in the **Number of copies** box then click **OK**.

PRINTING
Exercise 7.1: Printing

5. To obtain a Print Preview of the Sumner worksheet from the **7-1 Sales 1st Quarter.xls** workbook, open the **7-1 Sales 1st Quarter.xls** workbook in the **MOUS Excel 2000** folder, click the **Sumner** tab then click the ⌕ tool.

   To set the top margin to 5 cm (or 2 in), click the **Margins** button, then drag the second horizontal line downwards until you see the value **5** (or **2** if your unit of measurement is inches) appear on the status bar at the bottom of the Print Preview window.

6. To see a Web Page Preview of the **7-1 Aztec Charter.htm** Web page, open the **7-1 Aztec Charter.htm** document in the **MOUS Excel 2000** folder then use the **File - Web Page Preview** command.

7. To insert a page break between rows 13 and 14 of Sheet1 in the **7-1 Furniture.xls** workbook, open the **7-1 Furniture.xls** workbook in the **MOUS Excel 2000** folder then click the **Sheet1** tab.
   Click cell **A14** then use the **Insert - Page Break** command.

8. To create a print area for cells A5 to E18 of Sheet1 of the **7-1 Hi-Fi.xls** workbook, open the **7-1 Hi-Fi.xls** workbook in the **MOUS Excel 2000** folder then click the **Sheet1** tab.
   Select cells **A5** to **E18** then use the **File - Print Area - Set Print Area** command.

PRINTING
Lesson 7.2: Page Setup

- 1 ▪ Modifying page orientation 170
- 2 ▪ Changing the scale of printed pages 171
- 3 ▪ Printing a sheet with gridlines 171
- 4 ▪ Defining print quality 172
- 5 ▪ Defining printing margins 172
- 6 ▪ Creating page headers and footers 174
- 7 ▪ Repeating titles on each page 175

Practice Exercise 7.2 177

PRINTING
Lesson 7.2: Page Setup

1 ▪ Modifying page orientation

- If you are in the Print Preview, click the **Setup** button. Otherwise, use the **File - Page Setup** command.
- If necessary, activate the **Page** tab.
- Choose the appropriate **Orientation**.

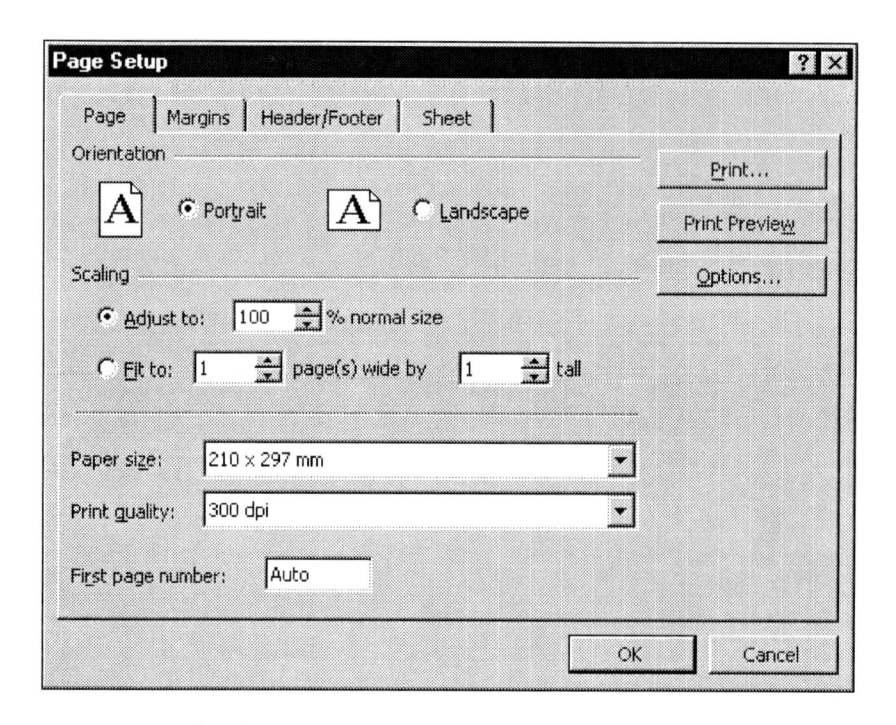

Portrait is also known as "Vertical" or "French". *Landscape* is also known as "Horizontal" or "Italian".

- Click **OK**.

2 ▪ Changing the scale of printed pages

- If you are in the Print Preview, click the **Setup** button. Otherwise, use the **File - Page Setup** command.
- If necessary, activate the **Page** tab.
- In the **Adjust to** text box, under **Scaling**, give the percentage of normal scale you wish to apply.
- Click **OK**.

> If the **Fit to** option is active in the **Page Setup** dialog box (**Page** tab), Excel automatically adjusts the scale of printing so that the document fits the number of pages (in width/height) you specify.

3 ▪ Printing a sheet with gridlines

- If you are in the Print Preview, click the **Setup** button. Otherwise, use the **File - Page Setup** command.
- If necessary, activate the **Sheet** tab.
- Activate the **Gridlines** option.
- Activate the **Row and column headings** option to print column letters and row numbers; deactivate it if you do not want these to be printed.
- Click **OK**.

PRINTING
Lesson 7.2: Page Setup

4 ▪ Defining print quality

- If you are in the Print Preview, click the **Setup** button. Otherwise, use the **File - Page Setup** command.
- If necessary, click the **Page** tab.
- Open the drop-down list for the **Print quality** option then click the desired resolution.

    This resolution corresponds to the number of points for each linear inch (ppi); the higher the resolution, the better the printed result. The resolutions available depend of the printer installed.

- Click **OK**.

5 ▪ Defining printing margins

- If you are in the Print Preview, click the **Setup** button. Otherwise, use the **File - Page Setup** command.
- If necessary, activate the **Margins** tab.

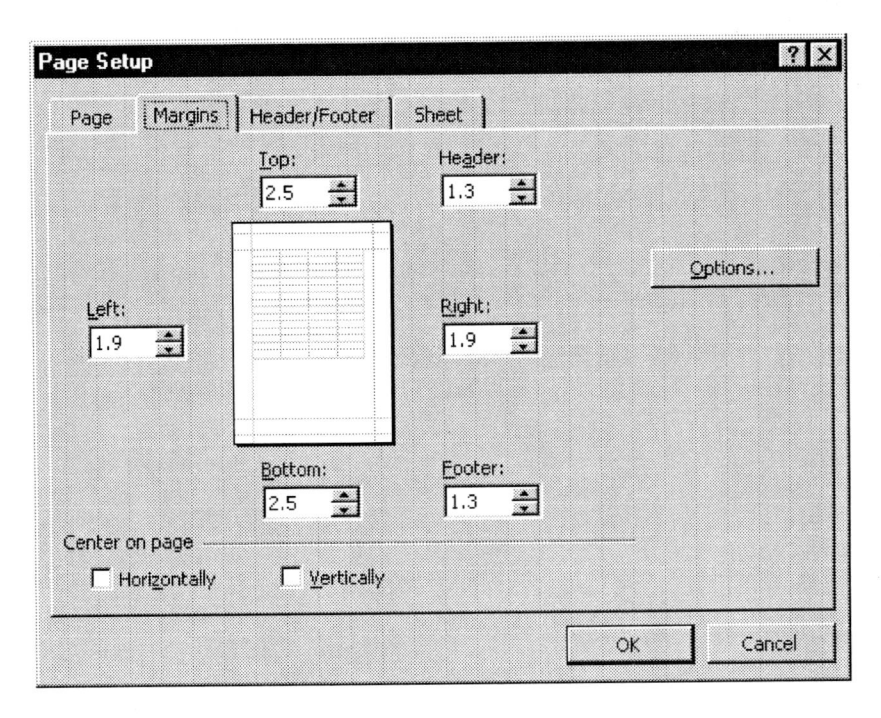

- Use the various text boxes to specify the corresponding margins. The **Header** and **Footer** options determine the position of the header text in the top margin and the footer text in the bottom margin.
- Activate the **Horizontally** and/or **Vertically** options to centre the table horizontally and/or vertically on the page.
- Click **OK**.

PRINTING
Lesson 7.2: Page Setup

6 ▪ Creating page headers and footers

The header is printed at the top of each page and the footer at the bottom of each page.

- If you are in the Print Preview, click the **Setup** button. Otherwise, use the **File - Page Setup** command.
- If necessary, activate the **Header/Footer** tab.

  You can also use the **View - Header and Footer** command.
- If you wish, you can select a pre-set **Header** and/or **Footer** from the corresponding list.

  Headers and footers chosen from the list are automatically centred at the top/bottom of the page.
- If necessary, you can create your own header and footer:

  - click the **Custom Header** and/or **Custom Footer** button.

  - activate the text box that corresponds to the required position on the page.

  - enter the text to be printed.
- To create a second (or third…) line of text, use the ⏎ key.
- To insert variable details, click the appropriate buttons:

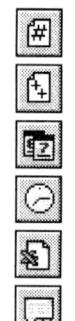

Button	Description
#	Page number
+	Total number of pages
📅	Date of printing
🕐	Time of printing
📄	File (workbook) name
📋	Tab (worksheet) name

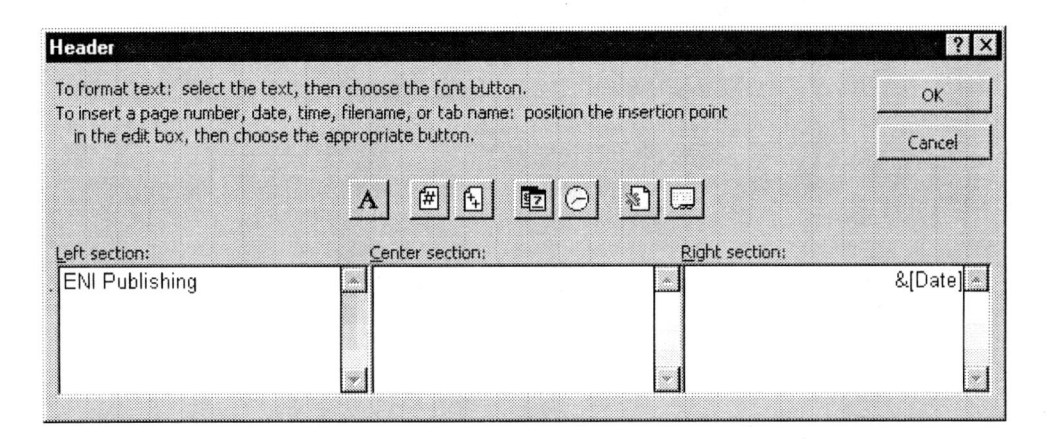

Each of these variables corresponds to a code which appears between square brackets.

* If you wish, you can format the text you have entered by selecting it and clicking the [A] button.
* Click **OK**.

Excel displays a preview of the header and footer as it will look in print.

* When you have defined your header and footer, click **OK**.

7 · Repeating titles on each page

Certain rows and/or columns (containing headings for example) can be repeated on each printed page.

* **File - Page Setup**
* If necessary, activate the **Sheet** tab.
* Activate the **Rows to repeat at top** box and/or the **Columns to repeat at left** box.
* Click the button to collapse the dialog box then on the worksheet select a cell in the row(s) and/or column(s) which you want to repeat.

PRINTING
Lesson 7.2: Page Setup

	A					F
	Print_Titles = PRODUCT					
2	Page Setup - Rows to repeat at top:				? X	
3	$4:$4					
4	PRODUCT	COST PRICE	SALE PRICE	PROFIT MARGIN	QUANTITY	PRO MA
5	Sofa bed	207	259	52	25	129
6	Sofa (3 seater)	449	539	90	18	161
7	Single bed	199	239	40	42	167
8	Double bed	399	519	120	58	694

In this example, row 4 containing the titles concerning the products, prices and margins will appear on each page printed.

- Click to expand the dialog box again then click **OK**.

MOUS
Excel 2000 Core

Below you can see **Practice Exercise** 7.2. This exercise is made up of 7 steps. If you do not know how to complete one of the steps, go back to the lesson to refer to the corresponding title. When you have finished, check your work by reading the **Solution** on the next page.

All the steps in this exercise are likely to be tested in the exam.

👉 Practice Exercise 7.2

1. Activate **Landscape** orientation for **Sheet1** of the **7-2 Furniture.xls** workbook in the **MOUS Excel 2000** folder.

2. Set the printing scale to **120%** for **Sheet1** of the **7-2 Furniture.xls** workbook in the **MOUS Excel 2000** folder.

3. Print the gridlines and the row and column headings for the **Taylor** worksheet in the **7-2 Loan.xls** workbook, located in the **MOUS Excel 2000** folder.

4. Define a print quality of **300 ppi** for the **Taylor** worksheet in the **7-2 Loan.xls** workbook, in the **MOUS Excel 2000** folder.

5. Modify the top margin to **3.5 cm** (or **1.2 in**) for **Sheet1** of the **7-2 Furniture.xls** workbook in the **MOUS Excel 2000** folder.

6. In **Sheet1** of the **7-2 Furniture.xls** workbook insert today's date in the right section of the header and the page number in the centre section of the footer.

PRINTING
Exercise 7.2: Page Setup

7. Repeat the titles in row **4** on each printed page of **Sheet1** of the **7-2 Furniture.xls** workbook in the **MOUS Excel 2000** workbook.

If you want to put what have learnt into practice on a real document, you can work on summary exercise 7 for the PRINTING section that you can find at the end of this book.

MOUS
Excel 2000 Core

It is often possible to perform a task in several different ways, but here only the quickest solution is presented. Go back to the lesson to see the other techniques that can be used.

Solution to Exercise 7.2

1. To print Sheet1 of the 7-2 Furniture.xls workbook in Landscape orientation, open the **7-2 Furniture.xls** workbook, in the **MOUS Excel 2000** folder then click the **Sheet1** tab.
   Use the **File - Page Setup** command then click the **Page** tab.
   Click the **Landscape** option in the **Orientation** frame then click **OK**.

2. To change the printing scale of Sheet1 in the 7-2 Furniture.xls workbook to 120%, open the **7-2 Furniture.xls** workbook and click the **Sheet1** tab.
   Use the **File - Page Setup** command then click the **Page** tab.
   Click the **Adjust to** box, enter **120** then click **OK**.

3. To print the cell gridlines plus the row and column headings for the Taylor sheet in the 7-2 Loan.xls workbook, open the **7-2 Loan.xls** workbook in the **MOUS Excel 2000** folder then click the **Taylor** tab.
   Use the **File - Page Setup** command then click the **Sheet** tab.
   Activate the **Gridlines** and **Row and column headings** options in the **Print** frame then click **OK**.

4. To set a print quality of 300ppi for the Taylor sheet in the 7-2 Loan.xls workbook, open the **7-2 Loan.xls** workbook in the **MOUS Excel 2000** folder then click the **Taylor** tab.
   Use the **File - Page Setup** command then click the **Page** tab.
   Open the **Print quality** list, click a resolution of **300ppi** then click **OK**.

PRINTING
Exercise 7.2: Page Setup

5. To set the top margin of Sheet1 of the 7-2 Furniture.xls workbook at 3.5 cm (1.2 in), open the **7-2 Furniture.xls** workbook in the **MOUS Excel 2000** folder and click the **Sheet1** tab.
Use the **File - Page setup** command then click the **Margins** tab.
Click the **Top** text box and enter **3.5** (or **1.2** if you use inches) then click **OK**.

6. To insert in Sheet1 of the 7-2 Furniture.xls workbook a date in the right of the header and a page number in the centre of the footer, open the **7-2 Furniture.xls** workbook in the **MOUS Excel 2000** folder then click the **Sheet1** tab.
Use the **File - Page Setup** then click the **Header/Footer** tab.
Click the **Custom Header** button then the **Right section**.
Click the [icon] tool then click **OK**.
Click the **Custom Footer** button then the **Center section**.
Click the [icon] tool then **OK**.
Click **OK** to confirm the changes made in the **Page Setup** dialog box.

7. To repeat the titles in row 4 on each printed page of Sheet1 of the 7-2 Furniture.xls workbook, open the **7-2 Furniture.xls** workbook in the **MOUS Excel 2000** folder then click the **Sheet1** tab.
Use the **File - Page Setup** command then click the **Sheet** tab.
Click the [icon] button on the **Rows to repeat at top** box then click cell A4 on the worksheet.
Click the [icon] button then **OK**.

DRAWING OBJECTS
Lesson 8.1: Charts

1 - Creating a chart in a worksheet 182

2 - Defining page setup for a chart 185

3 - Previewing a chart 186

4 - Printing a chart 187

5 - Activating/deactivating an embedded chart 187

6 - Selecting the different objects in a chart 188

7 - Changing chart type 190

8 - Inserting gridlines in a chart 191

9 - Modifying the display of tick mark labels 192

10 - Managing a chart legend 194

11 - Deleting a data series 194

12 - Adding a data series to an embedded chart 195

13 - Adding/deleting a data category 196

Practice Exercise 8.1 198

DRAWING OBJECTS
Lesson 8.1: Charts

1 ▪ Creating a chart in a worksheet

A chart can be inserted into a worksheet (to accompany a table for example).

- **Insert - Chart** or
- Select the **Chart type** then the **Chart sub-type**.
- Click the **Next** button.
- If all the data you need for the chart is contained in cells adjacent to one another, click the button under **Data Range** to select the range of cells on the worksheet. Use the **Rows** and **Columns** options to specify whether the series are in rows or columns. If the data needed for the chart are contained in cells that are not adjacent to one another, start by indicating whether the series are in **Rows** or **Columns** then activate the **Series** page.
  In the **Series** list, delete any series you wish to remove from the chart, using the **Remove** button.
  If necessary, redefine one or more series:

  - select the series and give its name: enter the name in the text box or click the **Name** box and select the cell containing the name you want to use.

  - give the references of the cells containing the values for the series: click the **Values** box to select its contents, click , select the values in the worksheet then click .
    Next, use the **Category (X) axis labels** option to specify which cells contain the text for the labels.

  Click the **Add** button if you need to insert further series.

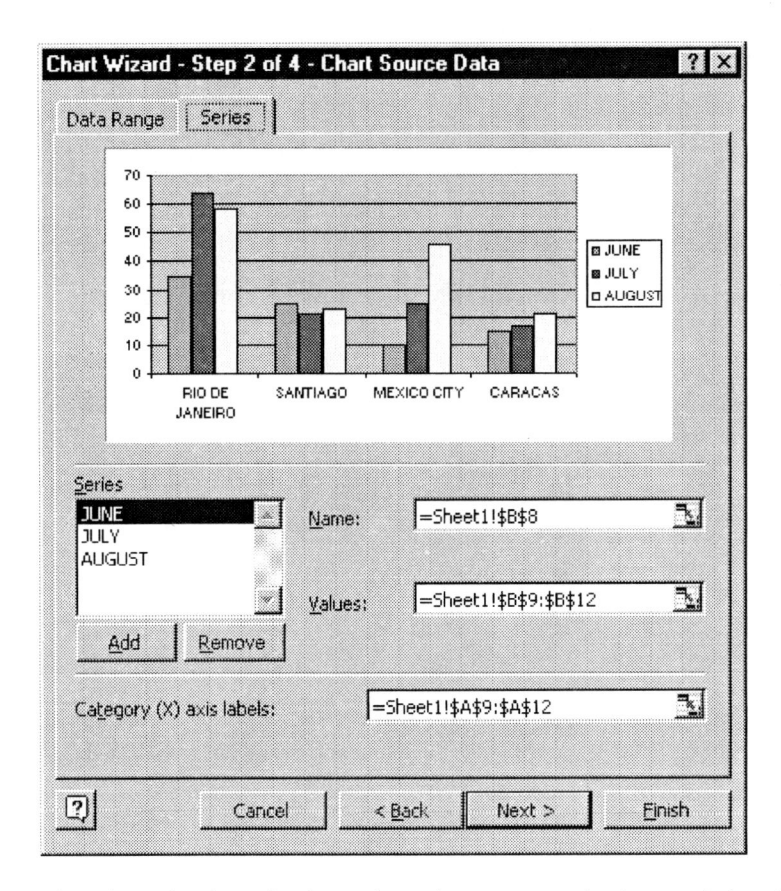

The chart displayed is based on the options which you defined.

- Click the **Next** button.
- In the text boxes on the **Titles** tab, give the various titles to be used in the chart.
- Click **Next**.
- If you wish to create the chart in its own chart sheet, activate the **As new sheet** option then give a name for the new sheet. Otherwise, leave the **As object in** option active and select the sheet where you want to insert the chart.
- Click the **Finish** button.

DRAWING OBJECTS
Lesson 8.1: Charts

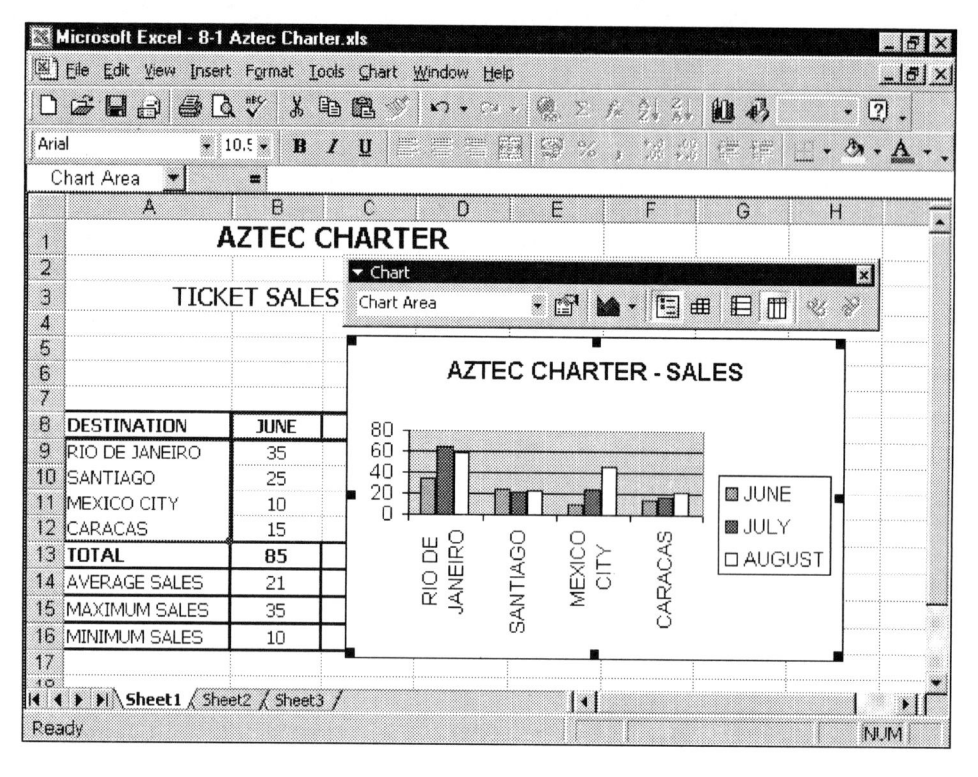

If you choose to insert the chart into a worksheet, it appears in the workspace. Small black squares, called handles, appear around it, showing that it is selected. A chart created within a worksheet is called an embedded chart.

When an embedded chart, created from data adjacent to it, is selected, colour-coded cell ranges appear. These show how the data from the worksheet have been used in the chart:
- data series are enclosed in a green rectangle
- categories are enclosed in a purple rectangle
- data points are enclosed in a blue rectangle.

Excel 2000 Core

- If necessary, move the chart as you would move any other drawing object: point to one of its edges then drag it. You can also resize the chart by dragging one of its handles.

> In a 2D chart, each series can contain up to 32000 points.
> By default, a chart is linked to its source data, so any changes made to the source data are automatically carried over into the chart.

Defining page setup for a chart

- Select the chart.
- If you are in Print Preview, click the **Setup** button. Otherwise, use the **File - Page Setup** command.

    The usual options on offer when printing worksheets are evidently not all available when you are working with a chart. The **Sheet** tab disappears but a new tab called **Chart** replaces it.

- In addition to the normal page setup options, you can also adjust the **printed chart size** under the **Chart** tab:

Use full page	distorts the proportions of the chart so that it fills the whole page.
Scale to fit page	increase the size of the chart as much as the page allows, without distorting its proportions.
Custom	prints a chart the same size as the chart on the screen.

- Click **OK**.

DRAWING OBJECTS
Lesson 8.1: Charts

3 ▪ Previewing a chart

- Select the chart if you want to preview only the chart: if you want to preview it along with the other data on the worksheet, click outside the chart.

- **File - Print Preview** or 🔍

    A scaled-down image of the sheet, as it will look when printed, appears.

- To zoom in on the preview, position the pointer over the area you want to magnify and click, or click the **Zoom** button.

    Before you click, the pointer takes the shape of a magnifying glass; once you are in zoom mode, it becomes an arrow.

- To return to the scaled-down sheet, click the page again or click the **Zoom** button.

- To display another page, use the **Next** and **Previous** buttons. When in the scaled-down version of the document, you can also use the vertical scroll bars to change page.

- To change the margins and column widths, click the **Margins** button.

- To manage page breaks on the active page, click the **Page Break Preview** button.

- To leave the Print Preview, click the **Close** button or press [Esc] on the keyboard.

4 - Printing a chart

- Select the chart.

  If you do not select the chart, any other information on the worksheet will be printed along with it.

- **File - Print** or `Ctrl` **P**
- Under **Print Range** activate the **All** option to print all the pages of the worksheet. If you want to print a certain number of pages, click the **From** box and enter the number of the first page to be printed then click the **To** box and enter the number of the last page you want to print.
- Leave the **Selected Chart** option active in the **Print what** frame.

  *In the **Print what** frame, the normal options available for worksheets (**Selection, Entire workbook**) are unavailable because the chart is selected.*

- In the **Number of copies** box, specify how many copies you wish to print.
- If you do not want multiple copies to printed in such a way as to simplify collation after printing (for example, pages 1,2,3 twice instead of 1 twice, then 2 and so on), deactivate the **Collate** option.
- Click **OK** to start printing.

5 - Activating/deactivating an embedded chart

- To activate an embedded chart, click it once to select the whole chart object then if necessary click to select one of the chart items.

  *The **Chart** menu replaces the **Data** menu.*

- To deactivate an embedded chart, click a cell in the sheet, outside the chart.
- To display an embedded chart in a window, select it then use **View - Chart Window**. Close this window to deactivate the chart.

DRAWING OBJECTS
Lesson 8.1: Charts

6 ▪ Selecting the different objects in a chart

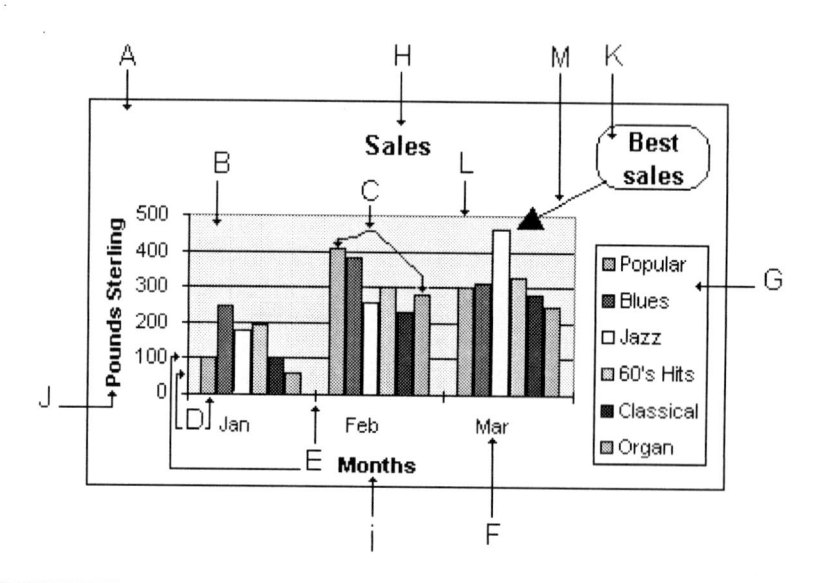

	object	to select	contents
A	Chart area	Click in the chart but not in any object	All the chart objects
B	Plot area	Click in the plot area but not in any object	The axes and data markers
C	Point	Click the series then click the point	Each value in a series
	Series	Click one of the data markers in the series	All the points that constitute a data series
D	Value Axis Category Axis	Click one of the tick mark labels	
E	Tick marks	No selection	Lines which divide up the axes

F	Tick mark labels	No selection	Texts attached to tick marks
G	Legend	Click the object	Shows the names of the series represented in the chart and identifies the symbol or colour used for the data markers
H	Chart title	Click the object	Attached text
I	Value axis title	Click the object	Attached text
J	Category axis title	Click the object	Attached text
K	Text box	Click the object	Unttached text
L	Gridlines	Click one of the lines	Lines crossing the plot area to make it easier to read the chart
M	Arrow	Click the object	

When you point to an object in a chart, its name and value appears in a ScreenTip, providing that the **Show names** option is active in the **Options** dialog box, **Chart** tab (**Tools - Options**). You can also select a chart object by opening the list box on the **Chart** bar and clicking the object's name.

DRAWING OBJECTS
Lesson 8.1: Charts

7 • Changing chart type

- Select the chart.
- **Chart - Chart Type**
- Choose the chart type required.

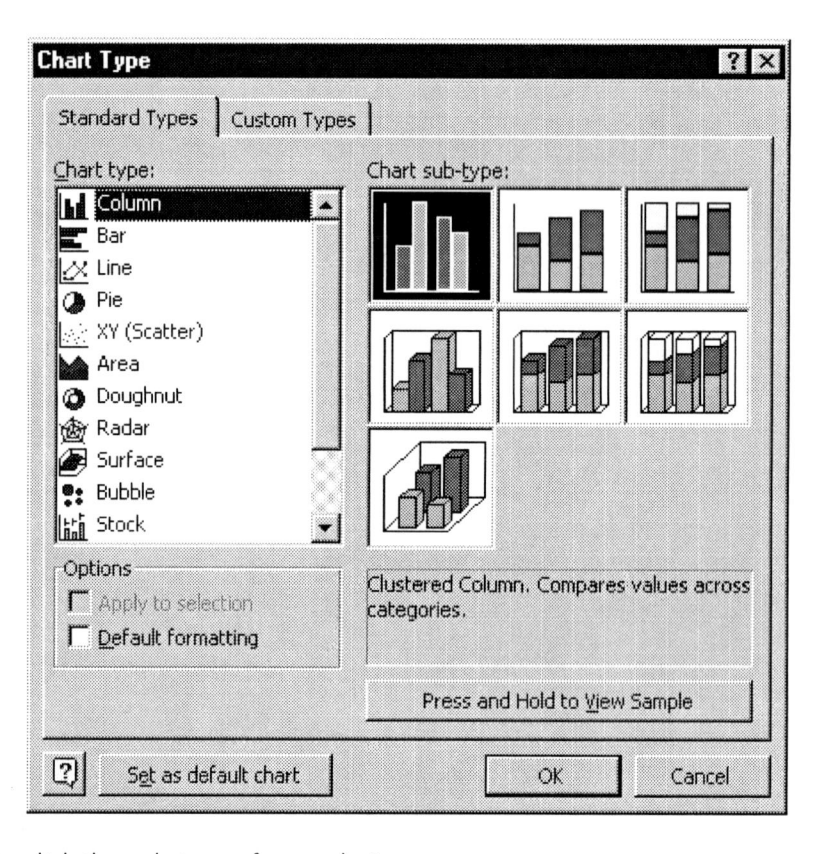

- Double-click the sub-type of your choice.

MOUS
Excel 2000 Core

The [icon] button on the **Chart** toolbar is used to change chart type but does not allow you to choose between the various sub-types.

The **Source Data** option in the **Chart** menu allows you to redefine the different series in the chart.

All the options for managing the chart can be found in **Chart - Chart Options**.

8 ▪ Inserting gridlines in a chart

- Select the chart.
- **Chart - Chart Options - Gridlines** tab
- Activate the options in the **Category (X) axis** frame to add vertical gridlines to the chart.
- Activate the options in the **Value (Y) axis** frame to add horizontal gridlines to the chart.

DRAWING OBJECTS
Lesson 8.1: Charts

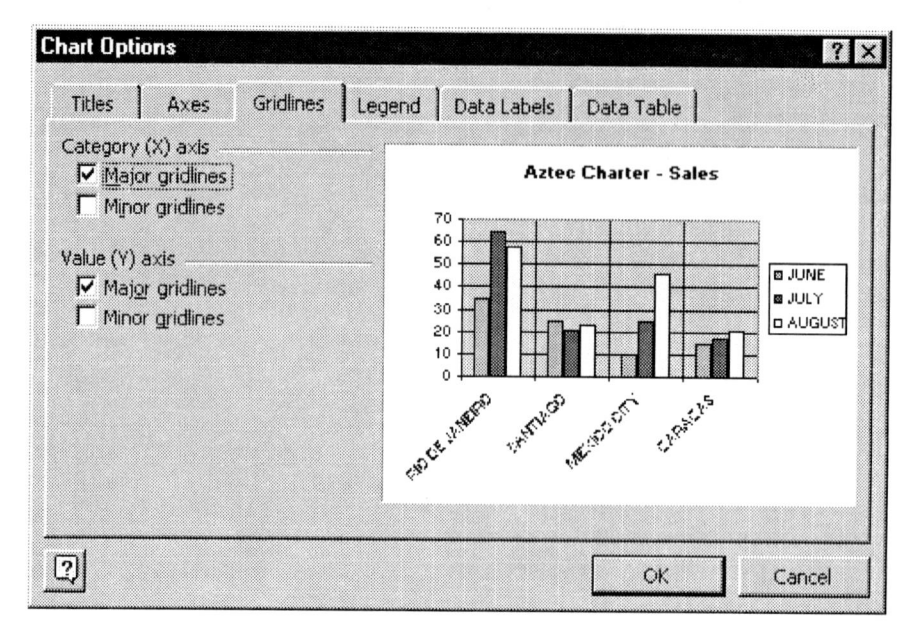

- Click **OK**.

9 • Modifying the display of tick mark labels

- Select the category axis whose tick mark labels need formatting.
- **Format - Selected Axis** or [icon] or Ctrl 1
- Use the **Font** and **Number** tabs to define the format of text and numbers in the labels.

* Define the position of the labels relative to the axis, using the options under the **Patterns** tab:

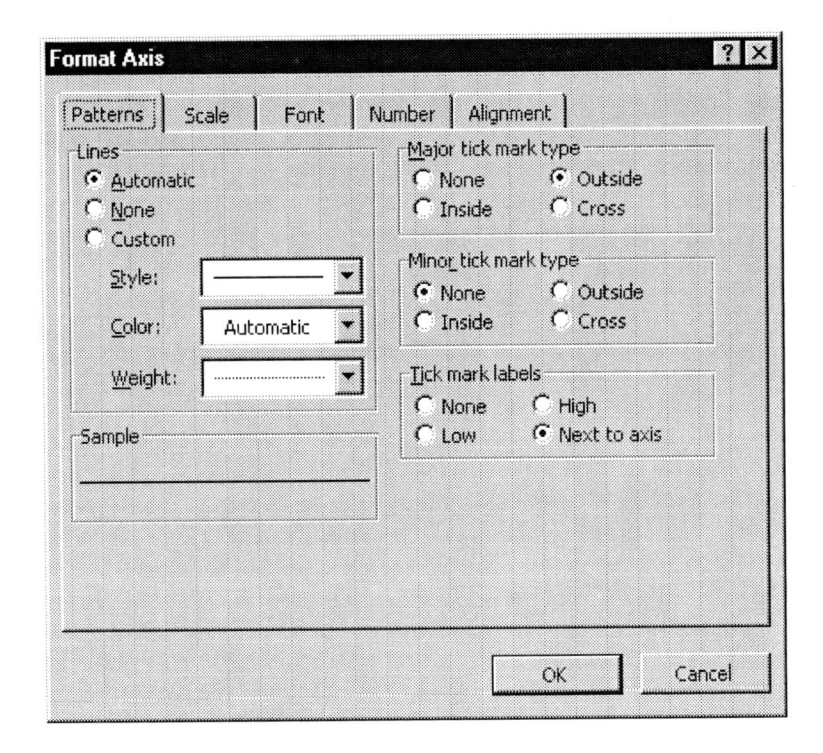

* On the **Alignment** page, determine the orientation of the text in the labels.
* Click **OK**.

  > *The* [icon] *and* [icon] *buttons on the **Chart** toolbar can be used to change the orientation of the text in the labels.*

DRAWING OBJECTS
Lesson 8.1: Charts

10 ▪ Managing a chart legend

- Click the [icon] button on the **Chart** toolbar to display or hide the legend.
- To define the legend's position, double-click the legend then activate the **Placement** tab:

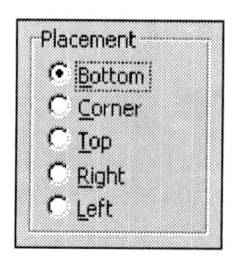

```
Placement
  ⦿ Bottom
  ○ Corner
  ○ Top
  ○ Right
  ○ Left
```

- In the **Placement** frame, double-click the position you require.

> 📄 *The legend is displayed horizontally when moved to the top or the bottom of the chart.*

> 🔍 *The legend can also be dragged to its new position.*

11 ▪ Deleting a data series

- Select the chart.
- **Chart - Source Data - Series** tab
- In the **Series** list, select the series you want to delete.
- Click the **Remove** button.

- Click **OK**.

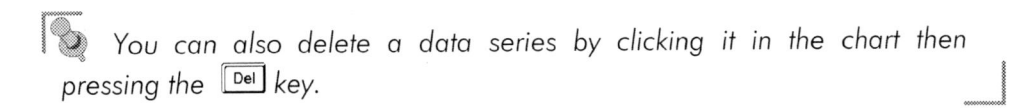

> You can also delete a data series by clicking it in the chart then pressing the [Del] key.

12 ▪ Adding a data series to an embedded chart

First method

This can only be used when the series to be added is next to the series already included in the chart.

- Select the chart area.

  On the worksheet, the cells containing the data series are enclosed in a green rectangle.

- Drag the handle of the green rectangle until it has encompassed the values of the new series.

Second method

- Select the cells containing the values corresponding to the series.
- Drag the selection onto the chart.

> This method is very quick but can only be used for embedded charts when the source data is close by. If the chart is in a chart sheet, you can copy the source data using the clipboard.

DRAWING OBJECTS
Lesson 8.1: Charts

Third method

- **Chart - Source Data - Series** tab
- Click the **Add** button.

    Excel creates a new series called series1.

- Click the **Name** box and give the new series a name.
- Click the **Values** box and click the ▨ button to work in the sheet. Select the cells containing the values for the new series and click the ▨ to restore the dialog box.
- Click **OK**.

    📄 *This command can also be used to change the cells associated with a series.*
    *You can also use the **Chart - Add Data** command.*
    If you wish to add a series or category to a chart sheet, you must select and copy the cells corresponding to the series or category then paste them into the chart sheet.

13 ▪ Adding/deleting a data category

Either the mouse or the menus can be used to add or delete a category in an embedded chart.

🖱 ▪ Select the chart area.
 ▪ To add a new category, and its corresponding data points, drag the handle of the purple rectangle until it encompasses the cells containing the new category. To delete a category, reduce the rectangle so the data in question is excluded from it.

> *This method can only be used in the case of an embedded chart, with the source data close by.*
> *If the category you wish to add is not adjacent to the existing categories, you can select the corresponding cells and drag them into the chart.*

- Select the chart area.
- **Chart - Add Data**
- In the **Range** text box, give the references of the data you want to add then click **OK**.

    The *Paste Special* dialog box may appear.

- If this occurs, activate the **New point(s)** option. In the **Values (Y) in** frame, indicate whether the series are in rows or columns. Activate the **Categories (X Labels) in First Column** option if the selected range contains category labels.
- Click **OK**.

DRAWING OBJECTS
Exercise 8.1: Charts

Below you can see **Practice Exercise** 8.1. This exercise is made up of 13 steps. If you do not know how to complete one of the steps, go back to the lesson to refer to the corresponding title. When you have finished, check your work by reading the **Solution** on the next page.

Steps that are likely to be tested on the exam are marked with a 🖽 symbol. It is however recommended that you follow the whole exercise in order to gain a complete understanding of the lesson.

☞ Practice Exercise 8.1

In order to complete exercise 8.1, you should open the **8-1 Aztec Charter.xls** workbook in the **MOUS Excel 2000** folder then activate **Sheet1**.

🖽 1. Insert the following chart under the table in worksheet **Sheet1**:

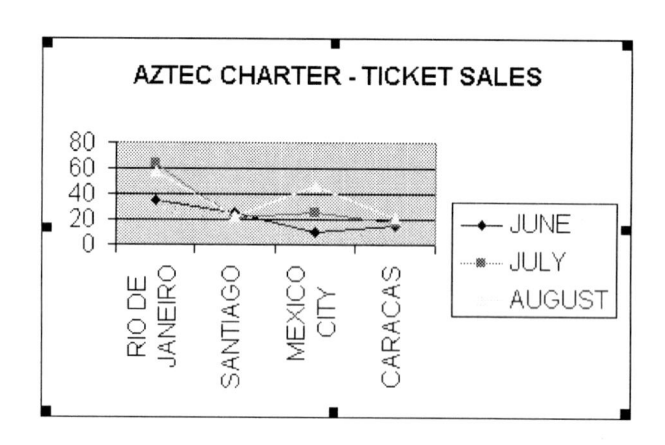

```
          AZTEC CHARTER - TICKET SALES
     80
     60
     40
     20                                    ──◆── JUNE
      0                                    ┄┄■┄┄ JULY
         RIO DE   SANTIAGO  MEXICO  CARACAS       AUGUST
         JANEIRO            CITY
```

🖽 2. Modify the chart's page setup so its size is adjusted to the page when printed.

🖽 3. Preview the chart as it would appear when printed, then close the Print Preview.

4. Print two copies of the chart.

5. Display the chart in its own window.

6. Select the chart title.

7. Change the chart type to a clustered column.

8. Add major gridlines to the value and category axes.

9. Change the font size of the category axis tick mark labels to **6 points**.

10. Display the legend above the chart.

11. Delete the **August** series from the chart.

12. Add the **August** series to the chart again.

13. Delete the **Caracas** data category from the chart.

If you want to put what have learnt into practice on a real document, you can work on summary exercise 8 for the DRAWING OBJECTS section that you can find at the end of this book.

DRAWING OBJECTS
Exercise 8.1: Charts

It is often possible to perform a task in several different ways, but here only the quickest solution is presented. Go back to the lesson to see the other techniques that can be used.

Solution to Exercise 8.1

1. To insert the chart, use the **Insert - Chart** command.
   Click the **Line** chart type then click first sub-type in the second column. Click **Next**.

   Under **Data Range**, click the button on the **Data Range** box, select cells **A8** to **D12** then click the button. Activate the **Columns** option, if necessary then click **Next**.
   Enter **AZTEC CHARTER - SALES** in the **Chart title** box then click **Next**.

   In the **As object in** box, leave **Sheet1** selected. Click the **Finish** button.

   Drag the chart area to place it underneath the table.

2. To make the chart adjust to one page when printed, click the chart to select it, use the **File - Page Setup** command and click the **Chart** tab.
   Click the **Scale to fit page** option under **Printed chart size** then click **OK**.

3. To preview the chart, select it then click the tool.
   Once you have viewed the chart, click the **Close** button to leave the Print Preview.

4. To print two copies of the chart, click the chart to select it then use the **File - Print** command.
   Enter **2** in the **Number of copies** box then click **OK** to start printing.

5. To show the chart in a separate window, click the chart to select it, then use the **View - Chart Window** command.

6. To select the chart title, click the **AZTEC CHARTER - SALES** text.

7. To change the chart type to a clustered column, click the chart to select it then use the **Chart - Chart Type** command.
   Select **Column** as the **Chart type** then choose the first **Chart sub-type** offered.
   Click **OK**.

8. To add major gridlines to the value axis and the category axis, click the chart to select it, use the **Chart - Chart Options** command then click the **Gridlines** tab.
   Activate the **Major gridlines** option in both the **Category (X) axis** and **Value (Y) axis** frames then click **OK**.

9. To change the font size to **6** on the category axis tick mark labels, click one of the tick mark labels on the Category axis (Rio, for example), use **Format - Selected Axis** then click the **Font** tab.
   Select the value in the **Size** box and enter **6** then click **OK**.

10. To display the legend under the chart, double-click the legend then click the **Placement** tab.
    Activate the **Bottom** option then click **OK**.

11. To delete the **August** series from the chart, click the chart to select it, use **Chart - Source Data** then click the **Series** tab.
    Select **August** in the **Series** list, click the **Remove** button then **OK**.

12. To add the **August** series back into the chart, select the chart area.
    Drag the green selection handle you can see at the bottom right of cell **C8** down to cell **D8**.

13. To delete the **Caracas** data category from the chart, select the chart area.
    Drag the purple selection handle you can see at the bottom right of cell **A12** upwards over cell **A11**.

DRAWING OBJECTS
Exercise 8.1: Charts

DRAWING OBJECTS
Lesson 8.2: Drawing objects

1 - Creating a drawing object 204

2 - Creating a text box 205

3 - Inserting a picture, sound or video 206

4 - Resizing/moving an object 208

5 - Selecting objects 208

6 - Changing an object's appearance 209

7 - Deleting objects 210

Practice Exercise 8.2 211

DRAWING OBJECTS
Lesson 8.2: Drawing objects

1 ▪ Creating a drawing object

Drawing an object

- Display the **Drawing** toolbar by clicking the ![tool] tool.
- Click the button that corresponds to the shape you wish to draw or click the **AutoShapes** button and choose one of the shapes given in the sub-menus.
- Drag to draw the shape on the workspace. Hold down the [Alt] key as you drag to align the object to the cell grid.

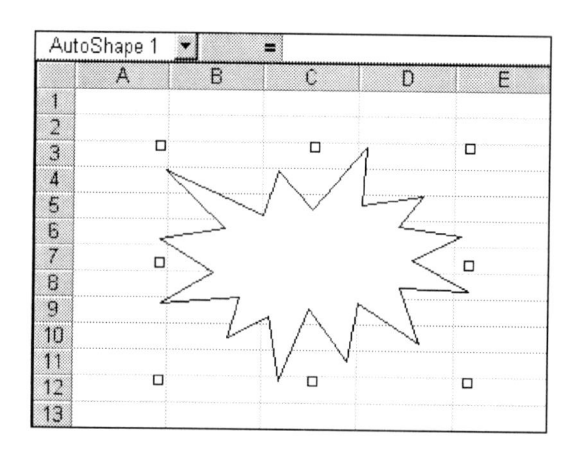

The name of the object drawn appears on the left of the formula bar.

Hold down the [Shift] key when you draw if you wish to make an evenly-proportioned square, circle or arc, or a perfectly horizontal, vertical or diagonal line.

Inserting a WordArt object

The WordArt application is used to apply special effects to text:

- Click the ![A] tool in the **Drawing** toolbar.
- Select an effect then click **OK**.
- Type the text to which you want to apply the WordArt effect; use the ↵ key when you want to create a line break.
- Use the **Font** and **Font Size** lists as well as the **B** and **I** buttons to format the text.
- Click **OK**.

The text appears on the worksheet as a drawing object.

> When a text object is selected, you can edit it using the tools from the **WordArt** toolbar.

2 ▪ Creating a text box

A text box is a drawing object that is designed to contain text.

- Click the ![icon] tool on the **Drawing** toolbar.
- Drag to draw the text box or click the place you wish to start entering the text. Use the Alt key as you drag if you wish to align the text box to the cell grid.

Once the text box has been created, an insertion point appears inside it.

- Enter your text, without worrying about line breaks. Use the ↵ key when you want to start a new paragraph.

DRAWING OBJECTS

Lesson 8.2: Drawing objects

6	Sofa (3 seater)	5%
7	Single bed	5%
8	Double bed	21%
9	Dining chair	2%
10	Folding chair	3%
11	Coffee table	2%
12	Square table	4%
13	Rectangular tab	6%
14	Wardrobe 2 do	4%

Following the January bedding promotion, sales of double beds account for 21% of sales, more than double the usual figure!

- If necessary, format the characters entered.
- Press [Esc] when you have finished your text.

3 ▪ Inserting a picture, sound or video

- **Insert - Picture - Clip Art**

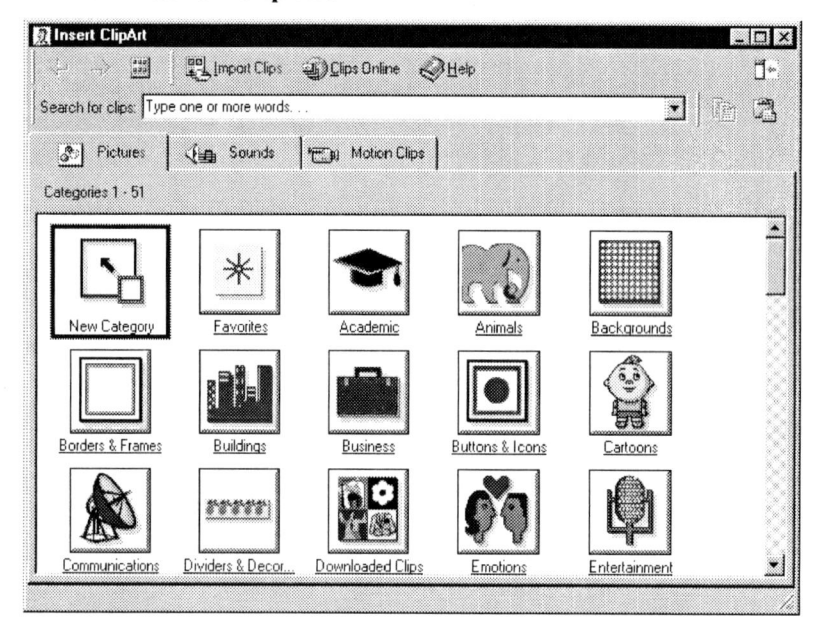

*The available categories of clip art appear on the **Pictures** page (there are 51 by default).*

- To look for pictures by keyword, enter one or more keywords in the **Search for clips** text box.

  Any clip art pictures corresponding to your search request appear in the bottom part of the window.

- Click the [ ] button to minimize the **Insert ClipArt** window or the [ ] button to maximize it.

- Click the picture you want to insert then click the [ ] button or drag the picture from the **Insert ClipArt** window onto the worksheet.

- Move or resize the picture inserted in the sheet as you would for any drawing object.

- If you do not want to insert any other pictures, close the **Insert ClipArt** window by clicking the [X] button.

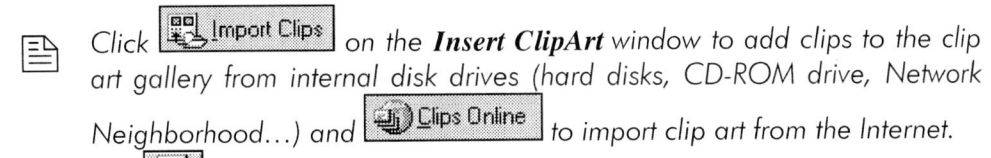

  Click [Import Clips] on the **Insert ClipArt** window to add clips to the clip art gallery from internal disk drives (hard disks, CD-ROM drive, Network Neighborhood...) and [Clips Online] to import clip art from the Internet.
  The [ ] button displays all the clip art categories.
  You can also insert sound and video clips by activating the **Sounds** and **Motion Clips** tabs on the **Insert ClipArt** dialog box.
  As with any drawing object, you can modify the background colour and borders of clip art pictures.

DRAWING OBJECTS
Lesson 8.2: Drawing objects

4 ▪ Resizing/moving an object

- Select the drawing object concerned.

  The black squares that appear around the selection are called **handles***. When you point to one of them, the pointer changes shape.*

- To resize an object, drag one of these selection handles.

  The current percentage of the object in relation to its original size can be seen in the **Name Box** *on the left of the formula bar.*

- To move an object, drag the object into its new position.

  Use the [Alt] *key as you drag to align the object with the cell grid.*

5 ▪ Selecting objects

- Click the [▸] tool on the **Drawing** toolbar.
- Click an object to select it.
- To select several objects, hold down the [Shift] key and click each object to select it.

  When several objects are selected, no name appears on the formula bar.

  You can also select several objects by dragging an invisible rectangle around them.

6 ▪ Changing an object's appearance

A 2D object

- Select the object.
- Use the buttons on the **Drawing** toolbar:

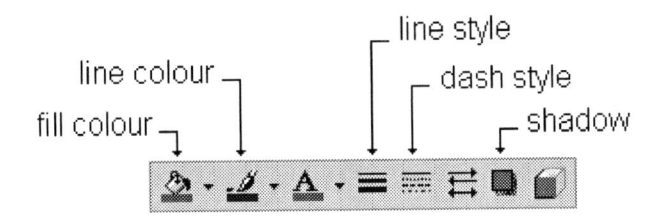

line style, line colour, dash style, fill colour, shadow

📄 The ⇄ button is used to define arrowheads for line objects.
To remove an object's borders, select it then choose **Format - Text Box - Colors and Lines** tab. Go into the **Color** list and choose the **No Line** option.

A 3D object

- Select the object then click the 🔲 button to select a pre-set 3D style. If none of these styles is suitable, click the **3D Settings** button to create a specific 3D effect:

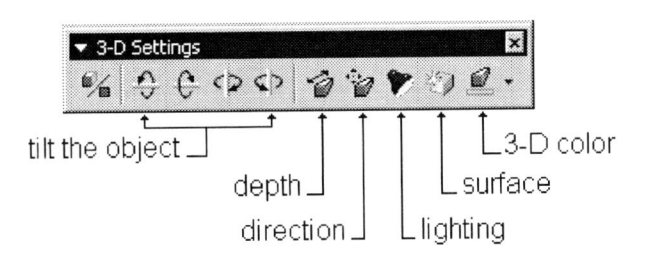

tilt the object, depth, direction, lighting, surface, 3-D color

DRAWING OBJECTS
Lesson 8.2: Drawing objects

> *Some of these effects can be found in the **Format AutoShape** dialog box: double-click the object to display this dialog box.*

7 ▪ Deleting objects

- Select the object(s) that you wish to delete.
- Press the Del key on the keyboard.

Below you can see **Practice Exercise** 8.2. This exercise is made up of 7 steps. If you do not know how to complete one of the steps, go back to the lesson to refer to the corresponding task. When you have finished, check your work by reading the **Solution** on the next page.

Steps that are likely to be tested on the exam are marked with a 🖽 symbol. It is however recommended that you follow the whole exercise in order to gain a complete understanding of the lesson.

☞ Practice Exercise 8.2

In order to complete exercise 8.2, you should open the *8-2 Furniture.xls* workbook in the **MOUS Excel 2000** folder then activate **Sheet1**.

🖽 1. Insert the text **Furniture World** as a WordArt object, placing the two words on separate lines. You should choose the Word Art effect located on the fourth row, in the fourth column.

🖽 2. Create the following text box, under the table (around cell C34):

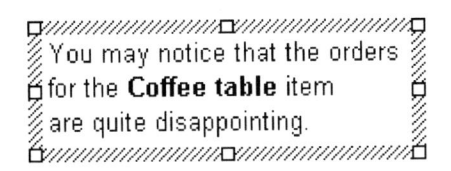

> You may notice that the orders for the **Coffee table** item are quite disappointing.

Remember to put the words Coffee table in bold type.

🖽 3. Insert into the worksheet the second picture (of a sofa) in the clip art category **Household**.

DRAWING OBJECTS
Exercise 8.2: Drawing objects

4. Resize the sofa picture keeping its proportions until it is 22% of its original size then move it towards cell **E2**.
   Next move the Furniture World object up so the table's title can be seen again.

5. Select the WordArt object (Furniture World) and the picture (the sofa).

6. Apply a yellow colour to the outline of the WordArt text (Furniture World), black to the text box border and red to the text within the text box.

7. Delete the picture of the sofa.

If you want to put what have learnt into practice on a real document, you can work on summary exercise 8 for the DRAWING OBJECTS section that you can find at the end of this book.

MOUS
Excel 2000 Core

It is often possible to perform a task in several different ways, but here only the quickest solution is presented. Go back to the lesson to see the other techniques that can be used.

Solution to Exercise 8.2

1. To insert the text **Furniture World** as a WordArt object, click the [4] tool then choose the fourth WordArt effect on the fourth row and click **OK**. Type **Furniture**, press ↵ on the keyboard, type **World** then click **OK**.

2. To create a text box, click the tool. Click cell **C34**, type the text **You may notice that the orders**, press ↵, type **for the Coffee table item**, press ↵ then type **are quite disappointing**.

   Select the words **Coffee table**, click the **B** tool then press Esc on the keyboard.

3. To insert the second clip art picture in the **Household** category, use the **Insert - Picture - ClipArt** command then click the **Household** category.

   Click the second image then the button.
   Click the ✕ button to close the **Insert ClipArt** dialog box.

4. To resize the picture (the sofa) to 22% of its original size, while keeping it in proportion, click the image to select it.
   Point to the bottom right handle on the picture then drag it until you can see **22% X 22%** in the **Name Box** on the left of the formula bar.

   To move the picture to cell **E2**, drag the picture into cell **E2**.

   To move the WordArt object (Furniture World) up so that the table's title can be clearly seen, click the WordArt object then drag it to the top of the worksheet.

DRAWING OBJECTS
Exercise 8.2: Drawing objects

5. To select the WordArt object (Furniture World) and the picture (the sofa), click the WordArt object, hold down the [Shift] key and click the picture.

6. To apply a yellow colour to the border of the WordArt object (Furniture World), click the WordArt object to select it.

   Open the list on the [tool icon] tool and click yellow.

   To apply black to the text box border and red to the text inside it, click the text box border to select.

   Open the list on the [tool icon] tool and click black.

   Open the list on the [A tool icon] tool and click red.

7. To delete the picture (the sofa), click the picture to select it then press the [Del] key.

SUMMARY EXERCISES

Summary 2 WORKBOOKS AND WORKSHEETS 216

Summary 3 ROWS, COLUMNS AND CELLS 217

Summary 4 MANAGING DATA 218

Summary 5 CALCULATIONS 219

Summary 6 PRESENTATION OF DATA 221

Summary 7 PRINTING 223

Summary 8 DRAWING OBJECTS 224

SUMMARY EXERCISES

Summary exercise 2 — WORKBOOKS AND WORKSHEETS

Open the **Chess club.xls** workbook in the **Summary** folder in the **MOUS Excel 2000** folder.

Give the name **Total** to **Sheet 3**.

Delete the **LEEDS** worksheet then move the **ABERDEEN** worksheet to after the **LONDON** worksheet.

Create a new table in the **TOTAL** worksheet (the first destination cell of the table should be cell **A4**) that will allow you to consolidate the data contained in the cell range **A6** to **C12** in worksheets **LONDON**, **ABERDEEN** and **PENZANCE**. This new table should display the sum of the values of these three sheets, include the row and column headings and be linked to the source data.

Send the **Chess club.xls** workbook by electronic mail as an attachment to the recipient(s) of your choice.

Save the changes you have made to the **Chess club.xls** workbook then close it.

A solution is saved under the name **Solution 2.xls** in the **Summary** folder.

Summary exercise 3 — ROWS, COLUMNS AND CELLS

Open the **STONES LTD customers.xls** workbook that is in the **Summary** folder of the **MOUS Excel 2000** folder, then modify the **Customers** worksheet as follows:

	A	B	C	Surname	Address	City	Postcode	Married
1				**CUSTOMER LIST**				
2								
3								
4								
5								
6								
7	Code	Name	Surname		Address	City	Postcode	Married
12	BAR001	James	Barnett	21 Oak Street	Fern Grove	4120	YES
13	BAR002	Julian	Barton	22 Harrison Avenue	Greerton	7520	YES
14	BLA001	Philip	Blake	14 Lingmoor Rise	Rafter	6250	YES
15	BRO001	Susan	Brown	2 Barncroft Mews	Abbeyville	8625	YES
16	BRO002	Wendy	Brown	14 King Street	St Lucia	5235	YES
17	BUT001	Adam	Butcher	13 Cannon Street	Westport	4101	NO
18	CAR001	Lucy	Carr	14 Harefield Rise	Killybill	9520	NO
19	CHE001	Gwen	Cheyne	13 Dean Avenue	Trout Lake	5280	YES
20	CLA001	Stewart	Clarke	51 Westfield Drive	Trout Lake	5260	NO
21	CLA002	Tony	Clarke	52 Cannon Street	Westport	4101	YES
22	CRA001	Beth	Crammond	45 Bethel Rise	Herston	4150	NO

Insert two rows after row **4**.

Delete rows **14** and **23** as well as column **B**.

Hide column **H**.

Change the width of column **A** to **9** and the height of row **7** to **30**.

Adjust the width of column **G** to fit its contents.

Freeze rows **1** to **7**.

Move cell **D56** in order to insert it between rows **57** and **58**.

A solution is saved under the name **Solution 3.xls** in the **Summary** folder.

SUMMARY EXERCISES

Summary exercise 4 — MANAGING DATA

Open the **STONES LTD orders.xls** workbook in the **Summary** folder of the **MOUS Excel 2000** folder and fill in the table in the **Jan - Apr** worksheet as shown below:

Order number	Customer code	Surname	Week no.	Order total	Sum paid	Sum outstanding
1	MIL001	MILLER	99 - 01	3,850	116	3,734.50
2	PIX001	PIXTON	99 - 01	2,575	77	
3	MCG001	MCGILL	99 - 02	1,185	36	
4	SIM001	SMITHERS	99 - 03	1,625	49	
5	LAN001	LANGLEY	99 - 04	1,570	47	
6	BAR002	BARTON	99 - 06	1,800	54	
7	GRE003	GREEN	99 - 07	635	-	
8	RAY001	RAY	99 - 12	790	-	
9	WIL001	WILSON	99 - 12	4,550	137	

Change the contents of cell **A10** to "**Order No.**".

Remove the format from cells **A6** to **B6**.

Copy the contents of cell **G11** to the adjacent cells **G12** to **G19**.

Move the contents of cell **A27** to cell **A24**.

Copy the format of cell **F10** to cell **F23**.

In cell **A24**, insert a hyperlink that allows you to open the **Solution 2.xls** workbook. The text for this hyperlink is **Click here to see customer list**.

Copy the contents of cell **G23** to cell **B5** in the **Recap Year** worksheet, and establish a link.

A solution is saved under the name **Solution 4.xls** in the **Summary** folder.

Summary exercise 5 — CALCULATIONS

Open the **Deliveries.xls** workbook stored in the **Summary** folder of the **MOUS Excel 2000** folder and complete the table in the worksheet **Sheet1** in order to produce the following results:

	A	B	C	D	E	F	G	H
8								
9	**Week no. 47**	North	East	South	West	TOTAL	% per driver	Bonus
10	Josh	10	25	30	25	90	6.61%	
11	Connor	15	20	60	16	111	8.15%	10.00
12	Michael	10	10	65	35	120	8.81%	10.00
13	Jack	12	50	70	70	202	14.83%	20.00
14	Tom	20	40	45	42	147	10.79%	10.00
15	Joe	15	15	80	20	130	9.54%	10.00
16	Steven	50	50	50	80	230	16.89%	20.00
17	Max	80	15	20	16	131	9.62%	10.00
18	Jonathan	15	20	40	18	93	6.83%	
19	Peter	20	30	45	13	108	7.93%	10.00
20	TOTAL	247	275	505	335	1,362		
21	Average	25	28	51	34			

Calculate the total deliveries for each area (B20 to F20) and for each driver (F10 to F19).

Calculate the average number of deliveries for each area (B21 to E21).

In cell **G10**, enter a calculation formula that allows you to calculate the percentage of deliveries made by driver **Josh**. Copy this formula for the other drivers (G11 to G19).

SUMMARY EXERCISES

In cells **H10** to **H19**, award a bonus of $20 to those drivers who have made 200 or more deliveries, and a bonus of $10 to those drivers who have made 100 or more deliveries. Those drivers who have made less than 100 deliveries will not receive a bonus.

Insert your computer's control date in cell **C5**; this date is not to be automatically updated when the workbook is opened.

A solution is saved under the name **Solution 5.xls** in the **Summary** folder.

MOUS
Excel 2000 Core

Summary exercise 6 — PRESENTATION OF DATA

Open the **Accounts.xls** workbook that is in the **Summary** folder in the MOUS Excel 2000 folder, and modify the **January** worksheet as shown below:

	A	B	C	D	E
1		**BUDGET JANUARY 2000**			
2					
3					
4					
5		Projected	Actual	%	Difference
6	**Income**				
7	Net earnings Mr	1,320	1,360	57.87%	40
8	Net earnings Mrs	900	920	39.15%	20
9	Family Allowance	70	70	2.98%	-
10	Total Income	2,290	2,350		60
11	**Expenditure**				
12	Rent	420	420	17.87%	-
13	Loans	350	350	14.89%	-
14	Taxes	195	195	8.30%	-
15	Insurance	57	57	2.43%	-
16	Electricty	125	110	4.68%	- 15
17	Telephone	55	68	2.89%	13
18	Savings plan	100	80	3.40%	- 20
19	Leisure	128	130	5.53%	2
20	Food & clothing	620	700	29.79%	80
21	School meals	70	70	2.98%	-
22	Transport	90	85	3.62%	- 5
23	Miscellaneous	80	85	3.62%	5
24	Total Expenditure	2,290	2,350		60

To cell **A1**, apply the font **Arial Black**, size **12**, then colour the characters dark blue.

Apply bold to cells **B5** to **E5**, **A10** and **A24**, and underline the contents of cells **A6** and **A11**.

Apply the fill **Gray - 25%** to cells **B5** to **E5**.

Centre the contents of cells **B5** to **E5** vertically and horizontally

SUMMARY EXERCISES

Copy the formatting from cell **B5** to cells **A6** and **A11**.

Apply a left indent of 2 characters to the text in cells **A7** to **A9** and cells **A12** to **A23**.

Merge and centre cells **A1** to **E1**.

Apply the **Percentage** format, with **two** decimal places, to cells **D7** to **D9** and **D12** to **D23**.

Create a style called **Label** by taking the format of cell **A6** and then apply it to cell **A24**.

Add borders to the table.

A solution is saved under the name **Solution 6.xls** in the **Summary** folder.

Summary exercise 7 — PRINTING

Open the **STONES LTD customers 2.xls** (which is a copy of the **Solution 3.xls** worksheet) in the **Summary** folder of the **MOUS Excel 2000** folder and prepare the **Customers** worksheet for printing:

Change the left and right margins to **1 cm** and reduce the scale to **95%** of the normal size.

In the right of the header the name of the workbook should be printed, and in the middle of the footer the number of the page, followed by a forward slash then the total number of pages should be printed.

Repeat the titles from row **7** on each page.

Insert a page break between rows **40** and **41**.

Have a look at the page set up using the Print Preview.

Print three copies of page **1**, then two copies of the cell range **A8** to **C52**.

A solution is saved under the name **Solution 7.xls** in the **Summary** folder.

SUMMARY EXERCISES

Summary exercise 8 — DRAWING OBJECTS

Open the **Toys.xls** workbook, found in the **Summary** folder in the **MOUS Excel 2000** folder, then activate the **1999** worksheet.

Create the column chart below from the table:

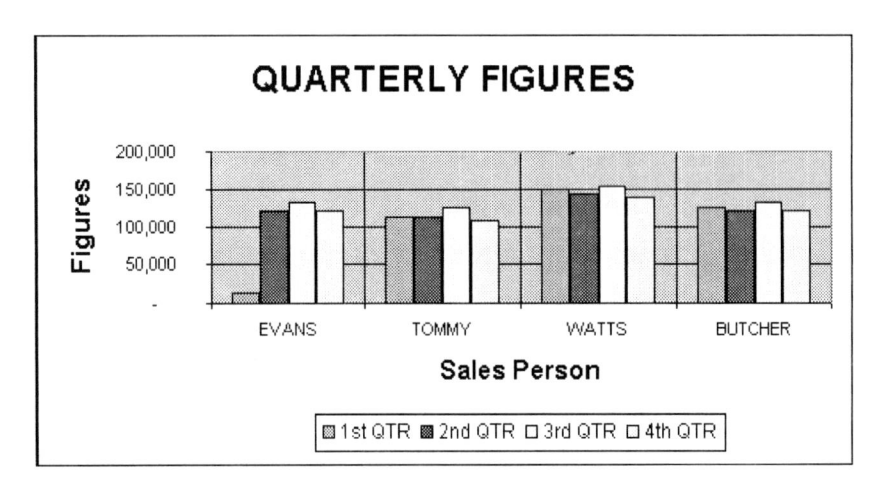

QUARTERLY FIGURES

(Column chart showing Figures on Y-axis from 0 to 200,000 for Sales Persons: EVANS, TOMMY, WATTS, BUTCHER across 1st QTR, 2nd QTR, 3rd QTR, 4th QTR)

This chart should be inserted as an object underneath the table in the **1999** worksheet; feel free to move and resize the chart.

Carry out the following actions, which will produce the chart in Solution 8:

- Change the size of the font of the labels on the category and value axes to **8**.
- Place the legend under the chart and apply size **9** to the legend text.
- Insert the major gridlines on the category axis.
- Add the **MARSTON** data series to the chart.

MOUS
Excel 2000 Core

Finish the chart by inserting the text box and arrow.

Print the chart; its size should adjust to fit the page when you print it.

A solution is saved under the name **Solution 8.xls** in the **Summary** folder.

TABLE OF OBJECTIVES

TABLE OF OBJECTIVES

Task	Lesson	Page	Exercise	Page
Working with cells				
Use Undo and Redo	Lesson 1.1 Titles 4 and 5	18	Exercise 1.1 Points 4 and 5	19
Clear cell content	Lesson 4.2 Title 2	84	Exercise 4.2 Point 2	90
Enter text, dates, and numbers	Lesson 4.1 Title 1	74	Exercise 4.1 Point 1	80
Edit cell content	Lesson 4.2 Title 1	84	Exercise 4.2 Point 1	90
Go to a specific cell	Lesson 3.2 Title 4	67	Exercise 3.2 Point 4	70
Insert and delete selected cells	Lesson 3.2 Titles 6, 7 and 8	68 and 69	Exercise 3.2 Points 6, 7 and 8	70
Cut, copy, paste, paste special and move selected cells, use the Office Clipboard	Lesson 4.3 Titles 1, 2, 3, 4, 5, 6 and 7	94 to 99	Exercise 4.3 Points 1, 2, 3, 4, 5, 6 and 7	101 and 102
Use Find and Replace	Lesson 4.2 Titles 4 and 5	85 and 87	Exercise 4.2 Points 4 and 5	90
Clear cell formats	Lesson 4.2 Title 3	85	Exercise 4.2 Point 3	90
Work with series (AutoFill)	Lesson 4.1 Titles 3 and 4	76 and 77	Exercise 4.1 Points 3 and 4	80
Create hyperlinks	Lesson 4.1 Title 5	78	Exercise 4.1 Point 5	80
Working with files				
Use Save	Lesson 2.1 Title 5	25	Exercise 2.1 Point 5	34
Use Save As (different name, location, format)	Lesson 2.1 Title 6	26	Exercise 2.1 Point 6	34
Locate and open an existing workbook	Lesson 2.1 Title 1	22	Exercise 2.1 Point 1	34
Create a folder	Lesson 2.1 Title 7	27	Exercise 2.1 Point 7	34

MOUS
Excel 2000 Core

Task	Lesson	Page	Exercise	Page
Use templates to create a new workbook	Lesson 2.1 Title 4	24	Exercise 2.1 Point 4	34
Save a worksheet/workbook as a Web Page	Lesson 2.1 Title 8	28	Exercise 2.1 Point 8	34
Send a workbook via email	Lesson 2.1 Title 10	30 to 33	Exercise 2.1 Point 10	35
Use the Office Assistant	Lesson 1.1 Title 2	16	Exercise 1.1 Point 2	19
Formatting worksheets				
Apply font styles (typeface, size, color and styles)	Lesson 6.1 Titles 1, 2 and 3	130 to 131	Exercise 6.1 Points 1, 2 and 3	145
Apply number formats (currency, percent, dates, comma)	Lesson 6.1 Titles 4 and 6	133 and 135	Exercise 6.1 Points 4 and 6	145
Modify size of rows and columns	Lesson 3.1 Title 7	59	Exercise 3.1 Point 7	61
Modify alignment of cell content	Lesson 6.1 Titles 7 and 8	135 and 136	Exercise 6.1 Points 7 and 8	145 and 146
Adjust the decimal place	Lesson 6.1 Title 5	134	Exercise 6.1 Point 5	145
Use the Format Painter	Lesson 6.1 Title 9	136	Exercise 6.1 Point 9	146
Apply AutoFormat	Lesson 6.1 Title 10	137	Exercise 6.1 Point 10	146
Apply cell borders and shading	Lesson 6.1 Titles 11, 12 and 13	138 to 141	Exercise 6.1 Points 11, 12 and 13	146
Merging cells	Lesson 6.1 Title 14	142	Exercise 6.1 Point 14	146
Rotate text and change indents	Lesson 6.1 Titles 15 and 16	143 and 144	Exercise 6.1 Points 15 and 16	147
Define, apply, and remove a style	Lesson 6.2 Titles 1, 2 and 3	152 and 153	Exercise 6.2 Points 1, 2 and 3	154

TABLE OF OBJECTIVES

Task	Lesson	Page	Exercise	Page
Page setup and printing				
Preview and print worksheets & workbooks	Lesson 7.1 Titles 1, 2, 3, 4 and 5	158 to 161	Exercise 7.1 Points 1, 2, 3, 4 and 5	165
Use Web Page Preview	Lesson 7.1 Title 6	162	Exercise 7.1 Point 6	165
Print a selection	Lesson 7.1 Title 3	159	Exercise 7.1 Title 3	165
Change page orientation and scaling	Lesson 7.2 Titles 1 and 2	170 and 171	Exercise 7.2 Points 1 and 2	177
Set page margins and centering	Lesson 7.2 Title 5	172 and 173	Exercise 7.2 Point 5	177
Insert and remove a page break	Lesson 7.1 Title 7	163	Exercise 7.1 Point 7	165
Set print, and clear a print area	Lesson 7.1 Title 8	164	Exercise 7.1 Point 8	166
Set up headers and footers	Lesson 7.2 Title 6	174	Exercise 7.2 Point 6	177
Set print titles and options (gridlines, print quality, row & column headings)	Lesson 7.2 Titles 3, 4 and 7	171, 172 and 175	Exercise 7.2 Points 3, 4 and 7	177 and 178
Working with worksheets & workbooks				
Insert and delete rows and columns	Lesson 3.1 Titles 2 and 3	54 and 55	Exercise 3.1 Points 2 and 3	61
Hide and unhide rows and columns	Lesson 3.1 Titles 4 and 5	56 and 57	Exercise 3.1 Points 4 and 5	61
Freeze and unfreeze rows and columns	Lesson 3.1 Title 6	58	Exercise 3.1 Point 6	61
Change the zoom setting	Lesson 1.1 Title 3	17	Exercise 1.1 Point 3	19
Move between worksheets in a workbook	Lesson 2.2 Title 2	41	Exercise 2.2 Point 2	48

MOUS
Excel 2000 Core

Task	Lesson	Page	Exercise	Page
Check spelling	Lesson 4.2 Title 6	88	Exercise 4.2 Point 6	90
Rename a worksheet	Lesson 2.2 Title 3	42	Exercise 2.2 Point 3	48
Insert and delete worksheets	Lesson 2.2 Titles 7 and 8	44	Exercise 2.2 Points 7 and 8	49
Move and copy worksheets	Lesson 2.2 Titles 4, 5 and 6	42 and 43	Exercise 2.2 Points 4, 5 and 6	48
Link worksheets & consolidate data using 3D References	Lesson 2.2 Titles 9 and 10	45 and 46	Exercise 2.2 Points 9 and 10	49
Working with formulas & functions				
Enter a range within a formula by dragging	Lesson 5.2 Title 1	116	Exercise 5.2 Point 1	124
Enter formulas in a cell and using the formula bar	Lesson 5.1 Title 1	106 and 107	Exercise 5.1 Point 1	111
Revise formulas	Lesson 5.1 Title 2	108	Exercise 5.1 Point 2	111
Use references (absolute and relative)	Lesson 5.1 Title 4	109	Exercise 5.1 Point 4	112
Use AutoSum	Lesson 5.1 Title 3	108	Exercise 5.1 Point 3	111
Use Paste Function to insert a function	Lesson 5.2 Title 3	118	Exercise 5.2 Point 3	124
Use basic functions (AVERAGE, SUM, COUNT, MIN, MAX)	Lesson 5.2 Title 1	116	Exercise 5.2 Point 1	124
Enter functions using the formula palette	Lesson 5.2 Title 4	119	Exercise 5.2 Point 4	124
Use date functions (NOW and DATE)	Lesson 5.2 Title 5	121	Exercise 5.2 Point 5	125
Use financial functions (FV and PMT)	Lesson 5.2 Title 6	121	Exercise 5.2 Point 6	125
Use logical functions (IF)	Lesson 5.2 Title 2	116	Exercise 5.2 Point 2	124

TABLE OF OBJECTIVES

Task	Lesson	Page	Exercise	Page
Using charts and objects				
Preview and print charts	Lesson 8.1 Titles 2, 3 and 4	185 to 187	Exercise 8.1 Points 2, 3 and 4	198 and 199
Use chart wizard to create a chart	Lesson 8.1 Title 1	182 to 185	Exercise 8.1 Point 1	198
Modify charts	Lesson 8.1 Titles 7, 8, 9, 10, 11, 12 and 13	190 to 197	Exercise 8.1 Points 7, 8, 9, 10, 11, 12 and 13	199
Insert, move, and delete an object (picture)	Lesson 8.2 Titles 3, 4 and 7	206, 208 and 210	Exercise 8.2 Points 3, 4 and 7	211 and 212
Create and modify lines and objects	Lesson 8.2 Titles 1, 2 and 6	204, 205 and 209	Exercise 8.2 Points 1, 2 and 6	211 and 212

A

ADJUSTING

Columns/rows to fit contents   60

ALIGNMENT

Horizontal   135
Vertical   136
See also ORIENTATION

APPLICATION

See MICROSOFT EXCEL

ATTACHMENT

Sending a workbook
as an attached file   32

AVERAGE

Using AVERAGE function   116

B

BORDER

Applying to cells   138

C

CALCULATION

Absolute cell references
in a formula   109
AutoSum   108
Copying results   97
Creating a formula   106
Making simple calculations
when copying   99
Modifying formulas   108
Statistical functions   116

CATEGORY

Adding to a chart   196
Deleting from a chart   196

CELL

Clearing contents   84
Clearing format   85
Definition   14
Deleting   69
Finding by contents   68
Going to a particular cell   40
Going to a specific cell   67
Inserting empty cells   68
Merging   142
Modifying borders   138

INDEX

Modifying contents 84
Moving cells then inserting them 69
See also ALIGNMENT, COLOUR, COPYING, FORMAT, MOVING, PATTERN, PRINTING, SELECTING

CHARACTER

See FONT, FORMAT, SIZE

CHART

Activating/deactivating 187
Adding a data category 196
Adding a data series 195
Changing type 190
Creating 182
Deleting a data category 196
Deleting a data series 194
Gridlines 191
Legend 194
Modifying tick mark labels 192
Page Setup 185
Previewing 186
Printing 187
Selecting chart objects 188

CLIPBOARD

See COPYING, MOVING

CLOSING

Workbook 30

COLOUR

Colouring cell background 140

Font colour 131
See also PATTERN

COLUMN

Adjusting width to contents 60
Deleting 55
Freezing/unfreezing 58
Hiding 56
Inserting 54
Modifying width 59
Repeating titles on each page 175
Selecting 54
Showing hidden columns 57

CONSOLIDATING

Worksheet 45

COPYING

Calculation results and formats 97
Cell contents to adjacent cells 94
Cells 94
Formats 136
Linking cells during copying 98
Making simple calculations when copying 99
Sheet into a workbook 42
Sheet into another workbook 43
Transposing data while copying 98
With the Office clipboard 96

COUNT

Using COUNT function 116

FOLDER

Creating	27

D

DATA

See ENTERING, FORMAT, MODIFYING

DATA SERIES

Adding to a chart	191
Creating	76
Creating a custom series	77
Deleting from a chart	194

DATE

Entering	74
Formats	135
Inserting control date	121

DECIMALS

See NUMERICAL VALUE

DELETING

Cell contents	84
Cell format	85
Cells	69
Drawing object	210
Rows/columns	55
Sheets	44

DOCUMENT

See WORKBOOK

DRAWING OBJECT

Changing a 2D object's appearance	209
Changing a 3D object's appearance	209
Creating	204
Deleting	210
Resizing/moving	208
Selecting	208

See also TEXT BOX, WORDART

E

EDITING DATA

See MODIFYING

ELECTRONIC MAIL

Sending a sheet/workbook	30
Sending a workbook as an attached file	32
Sending a workbook as the body of a message	30

ENTERING DATA

Several lines of text in one line	76
Text, values, dates	74

233

INDEX

ERROR

   See UNDOING

F

FILE

   See WORKBOOK

FILL HANDLE

   Definition   15

FINDING

   Cell with a particular content   85

FONT

   Modifying character font   130

FOOTER

   Creating   174

FORMAT

   AutoFormat   137
   Clearing from cell   85
   Copying   105
   Copying formatting   136
   Dates   135
   Indenting text   144
   Numerical values   133
   Text attributes   131

   See also ALIGNMENT, DRAWING OBJECT, FONT, ORIENTATION, SIZE

FORMULA

   Creating   106
   Including absolute cell references   109
   Modifying   108
   See also CALCULATION

FORMULA BAR

   Description   13

FORMULA PALETTE

   Using to insert a function   119

FUNCTION

   Pasting into a formula   118
   Using financial functions   121
   Using statistical functions   116
   Using the IF function   116
   See also COUNT, FV, IF, IPMT, MAX, MIN

FV

   Using the FV function   121

234

G

GRIDLINES

Adding to chart — 191
Printing cell gridlines — 171

H

HEADER

Creating — 174

HELP

Looking for help on the Web — 17
See also OFFICE ASSISTANT

HIDING

Rows and columns — 56

HYPERLINK

With another document — 78

I

IF

Using IF function — 116

INSERTING

Cells — 98
Control date — 121
Existing cells — 69
Function into a formula — 118
Function with the formula palette — 119
Rows and columns — 54
Sheets — 44

IPMT

Using the IPMT function — 122

L

LEGEND

See CHART

LINE

Entering several lines of text in one cell — 76

INDEX

LINK

Establishing between cells while copying	98
Establishing between worksheets	50
Linking worksheets	46

M

MARGIN

Defining	172
Modifying	161

MAX

Using MAX function	116

MERGING

Cells	142

MICROSOFT EXCEL

Application window	12
Starting/Leaving	12
Workbook window	14

MIN

Using MIN function	116

MODIFYING

Cell contents	84
Formula	108

MOVING

Cells	94
Drawing object	208
Existing cells	69
Finding a cell by its contents	68
From one sheet to another	41
Going to a particular cell	40
Going to a specific cell	67
Sheet to another workbook	43
With the Office clipboard	96
Worksheet	42

N

NAME

Naming a sheet	42

NUMBER

See NUMERICAL VALUE

NUMERICAL VALUE

Entering	74
Formatting numerical values	133
Modifying the number of decimal places	134

O

OFFICE ASSISTANT

Changing its look	16
Deactivating	17
Hiding	17
Showing	16

OFFICE CLIPBOARD

See COPYING, MOVING

OPENING

Workbook	22

ORIENTATION

Changing text orientation	143
Printed page	170

P

PAGE

Managing page breaks	163
Printing a group of pages	158
Repeating titles on each page	175

See also ORIENTATION

PAGE SETUP

See also MARGIN, ORIENTATION, PRINTING

PATTERN

Applying to cell background	140

PICTURE

Inserting	206

PREVIEW

Print preview	171
Web Page	162

PRINT AREA

Creating	164

PRINT PREVIEW

Using	160

See also CHART, PREVIEW

PRINTING

Cell gridlines	171
Cells	159
Group of pages	158
Margins	172
Printing scale	171
Quality	172
Repeating titles on each page	175
Several copies	160
Sheets	159

INDEX

Whole workbook 159
Worksheet 158
See also CHART, MARGIN, PAGE, PREVIEW, PRINT AREA

R

REPLACING

Cell contents 87

RESIZING

Drawing object 208

ROW

Adjusting height to contents 60
Deleting 55
Freezing/unfreezing 58
Hiding 56
Inserting 54
Modifying height 59
Repeating titles on each page 175
Selecting 54
Showing hidden rows 57

S

SAVING

A sheet/Workbook as
a Web page 28
Workbook 25
Workbook under another name 26

SCALE

Printing scale 171

SELECTING

Adjacent cells 66
All cells 67
Drawing object 208
Non-adjacent cells 66
Rows and columns 54

SENDING

See ELECTRONIC MAIL

SHEET

Copying into a workbook 42
See also ELECTRONIC MAIL, PRINTING, WEB PAGE

SHOWING

Hidden rows and columns 57

SIZE

Modifying character size 130
See also DRAWING OBJECT

SOUND
Inserting 206

SPELLING
Checking 88

STATUS BAR
Description 13

STYLE
Applying 153
Creating 152
Modifying/Deleting 153

SUM
Using AutoSum 108
Using SUM function 116

T

TAB
Definition 15

TEMPLATE
Creating a workbook from a template 24

TEXT
Entering 74

TEXT BOX
Creating 205

TICK MARKS
Modifying labels 192

TITLE BAR
Description 13

TRANSPOSING
While copying data 98

U

UNDOING
Redoing cancelled actions 18

V

VALUE
Entering 74

VIDEO
Inserting 206

VIEW
Showing an open workbook 23

INDEX

W

WEB PAGE

Preview	162
Saving a sheet/workbook as a Web page	28

WINDOW

Freezing/unfreezing panes	58

WORDART

Inserting	204

WORKBOOK

Closing	30
Created from a template	24
Creating	24
Opening	22
Saving	25
Saving under another name	26
Showing an open workbook	23

See also ELECTRONIC MAIL, PRINTING, WEB PAGE

WORKSCREEN

Application window	12

WORKSHEET

Consolidating	45
Copying into a workbook	41
Creating links	46
Deleting	44
Going from one sheet to another	41
Inserting	44
Moving	42
Moving around within cells	40
Moving/copying into another workbook	43
Naming	42

See also ELECTRONIC MAIL, PRINTING, WEB PAGE

Z

ZOOM

Changing magnification (zoom)	17

ENi Publishing

▲ Quick Reference Guide ▲ Practical Guide ▲ Microsoft® Approved
▲ User Manual ▲ Training CD-ROM Publication

VISIT OUR WEB SITE http://www.editions-eni.com

Ask for our free brochure

For more information on our new titles please complete this card and return

Name: ....

Company: ....
Address: ....
....
Postcode: ....
Town: ....
Phone: ....
E-mail: ....

Please affix stamp here

ENI Publishing LTD

500 Chiswick High Road

London W4 5RG